PRAISE FOR
QUINTON'S MESSAGES

Authentic Story of Transformation and Growth

We construct identities and tell stories to ourselves and others that become our realities. For Ernie Jackson, the passing of his son triggered an awakening and transformation in a way he understands himself, his family and the world that he/we all share. A keenly felt personal story that carries profound lessons for all of us.

Brian Dennis on Amazon – September 22, 2011

Great Book

I found out about Quinton through a link to a video of Ernie discussing his book. It was really well written and informative and so honest. When my daughter passed, like Ernie, I spent the first few weeks reading books by mediums and parents who had lost children before I tried to achieve contact with my daughter. I also waited until I had received signs from her that she was still around. Although, my experiences have been very real to me, reading about others who have had the same or similar experiences just makes it even more real. It reconfirms our knowing that our loved ones are still close and we will be with them again. Thank you, Ernie, for writing this book.

Barbara Lauman on Amazon – June 14, 2012
Author of Conversations with my Daughter on the Other Side

Please Read This Book

I highly recommend this book. As someone who has long questioned my own purpose, the message within this book hit hard and fast. Writing a book about his experiences was never in the cards for Ernie... or so he thought. I sat in the audience of Quinton's service and felt his presence. I had never met this sweet boy in the physical realm, but could see and feel his presence that warm summer day in 2009. I wept throughout my reading of Quinton's Messages, thinking of my loved ones who could benefit from the messages the book contains. I encourage you to read the book with an open mind and open heart. Who knows what you may discover in the process.

Kelly Cook Buszkiewic on Amazon – October 7, 2011

A Really Good Book to Read

This is one of those books that captures you form the first page. The author has a writing style that just brings you along as he recounts a tragedy that nobody should ever have to endure. I found myself completely engrossed and was surprised at how fast I finished the book. Upon completing it I couldn't help but feel sympathy for the author and his family and was left pondering unanswerable questions related to why bad things happen to good people.

As I continue to think about Quinton's Messages though, I have discovered that this really is a story about family, love and life. Reading it has proved to be a catalyst that has helped me to appreciate my family and to recognize what is really important in life. There are not many books that can have such an effect on people and Quinton's Messages is a book that I highly recommend.

Amrath on Amazon – December 11, 2011

Quinton's Messages – I got the message!

Really enjoyed the book and the perspective of family and friends throughout the book. Thank you or sharing your insights, not only am I more cognizant of my surroundings but also of my time and what is important.

MaryLynne on Amazon – October 21, 2013

Best Book of the Year

It took me less than two days to read this book cover to cover. It is one of the most touching, inspiring books I have ever read. Instead of dwelling on the day his son died, Ernie Jackson celebrates his son's life, and shows that when your loved ones pass from this life, that are not gone from us. The energy of their love is so great and they stay with us. To me, this is by far the best book of the year.

Paula Trigg on Amazon – December 7, 2011

Huge Impact!

Quinton's messages came across loud and clear in this powerful book, lovingly written by his father, Ernie Jackson. I have rarely finished a book that left me with such a clear and compelling takeaway message: There is far more going on than we are able to see or understand from our limited vantage point. Quinton's startling and dramatic transition was a wake-up call to his family and the rest of us to treat ourselves and each other with compassion. We are part of something larger and more significant than we can ever know. Thank you to Q for his messages and to Ernie for sharing them with the rest of us.

Kathey on Amazon – June 5, 2012

This Book is a Must Read!!

This has been the most influential book of my life. I recognize so much of me in the first part of the book as I related to Ernie prior to Quinton's passing and feared I would not get the message without a life changing event. After having read the book and many discussions with Ernie. I am proud to say that I have made very positive steps forward with my family and my spirituality. This book is a must read for all parents.

Julie Pate-Gurule on Amazon – December 3, 2012

From the Heart

This is my first book review. I realized this book was so powerful, so inspiring, so enlightening that it summoned me to participate.

Quinton's Messages will inspire you to be a better person in many facets of life. It will open doors to a bigger picture for you. You will walk in Quinton's footsteps, illustrated with heartfelt verbiage that only a father could pen. You will be moved, connected and "in the moment" every step of the journey with Quinton, Ernie and his family and dear friends. This is a life story, unfortunately colliding with tragedy, but the messages beyond the tragedy live forever. Thank you for moving me and opening doors, Ernie Jackson.

Blakester on Amazon – March 8, 2012

Truly life changing

This book is truly a confirmation of my faith in God and in people. What is most amazing to me is that I never met this angel Quinton, but his messages have changed my view of life, the way I live it and how I engage with others. I can see his messages everywhere! I have always believed that my mother who passed almost 10 years ago was with me all the time, but after reading Quinton's Messages, I now know that my mothers presence is REAL and not just me longing for more time with her. There truly is an entire world that exists beyond what we can only see. After reading this book, you will be convinced of this too! It will change your life…if you let it!

Awesome Book!

Beautifully written; powerful message! Ernie Jackson has shared the essence of a father/son bond that transcends this life on earth, taking the reader on a journey that gives deeper meaning to life as we know it. As the author delves into a higher purpose for his own life, one begins to realize that Quinton's messages are not only for the Jackson family, but are lessons applicable to each of us. We are given a gift from a grieving father: the gift of hope in a time of tragedy, the gift of love that over shadows death and the chance to cherish the angels walking among us.

Deep

I learned of this book after my brother and sister-in-law were in a horrific accident. Although they both survived, they and their children have a new normal. Coincidentally, my sister-in-law knows Ernie and his family. I was lucky enough to meet him and feel his passion. I feel and look at things differently since I read this book, looking at life with a fresh perspective. I have recommended this book numerous times. Thank you.

One family's life changing experiences leads to life changes for those willing to listen

The Jackson family's tragedy resonates deeply in this fast paced telling of their experiences before and after the death of their son. The book contains several themes which easily translate to the lives of families all over the world. For me, the father of a 19 month old son, I was touched and affected by Ernie's telling of the events prior to and after the accident, I would recommend this to anyone searching for answers in life but too busy to simply look around them. The book touches mind, body and spirit along the Jackson family's journey. Ernie's recollections of his son make you smile, even laugh out loud as he attempts to share Quinton's life and spirit. I've passed this onto my own father with the hopes that we can reconcile some of our own differences and make peace with the fact that this life and this world is much larger than we tend to believe it is. 100% recommended.

MVP on Amazon – April 26, 2012

Must Read

This book is a must read for any and all who have questions about what happens to us when we die. Is it truly a better place? Do our loved ones miss us, still love us, remember us? This book has already helped so many people struggling with the loss of a loved one. This book is truly a must read for all of us who've lost someone we love. I could not put it down and you won't either. I've already given this book as a gift to several folks who were struggling through loss. It is a perfect gift at a tough time; very well written page turner that I will continue to gift people suffering and in need. You will not be disappointed!

Debbie on Amazon – December 10, 2012

Do yourself a favor and read this book!

I personally experienced the loss of my 2 year old nephew in 2007. I have seen the pain that my sister and brother-in-law have experienced as a result of their child's death. This said, I can only imagine the pain that Ernie Jackson and his family have experienced over the past couple of years due to the loss of their beloved son. Quinton's Messages is a must read for everybody as it gives a message of hope and is a reminder how precious life is, and that we need to live each day to the fullest.

I had the opportunity of personally meeting Ernie Jackson and told him that after reading Quinton's Messages, I felt as though I knew his entire family. Mr. Jackson has opened himself up in this book and gives detailed stories from his childhood, college years and family vacations.

Quinton's Messages is written in a way that makes the reader continually ask themselves, "what is going to happen next?" In fact, I read this book in a single day as I was unable to put it down. I highly recommend this book to anyone who is simply looking for a good read. Be warned though… You will experience the full gamut of emotions.

Matt S. on Amazon – March 21, 2012

Quinton's Messages

ISBN: 978-0-9863442-4-4

www.quintonsmessages.com

Book design by Bella Media Management

Printed in the United States of America.

Second Edition

Note from the Author – Special thanks to Lindsay Cullen and Jan Whalen of Whalen Voices LLC who made this 2nd edition of Quinton's Messages possible. Your work identifying typos and grammatical opportunities for improvement will forever be appreciated. Also, Thank you Carol Web of Bella Media Management (www.bellamediamanagement.com) for the cover, layout and uploading the second edition of Quinton's Messages.

To contact Ernie or Kristine Jackson, e-mail stonejak4@hotmail.com or Ernie@quintonsmessages.com.

QUINTON'S MESSAGES

SECOND EDITION

ERNIE JACKSON

DEDICATED TO OUR SON,
QUINTON STONE JACKSON.

Thank you for showing me how to live and how to love.

TABLE OF CONTENTS

Introduction   i

Chapter One: Found and Lost Again   1

Chapter Two: Quinton Stone Jackson   11

Chapter Three: Our Vacations: Respites from the Agony   31

Chapter Four: Vacation 2009   41

Chapter Five: The End of the Vacation   69

Chapter Six: The Hospital Stay   79

Chapter Seven: The Week of June 12   97

Chapter Eight: Going Home   109

Chapter Nine: The Service   117

Chapter Ten: Summer of 2009   125

Chapter Eleven: Quinton's Visits   133

Chapter Twelve: Quinton's Messages   155

Chapter Thirteen: What Happens When Our Loved Ones
Transition   159

Chapter Fourteen: Who We Were   181

Summary   203

Afterward   211

Acknowledgememnts   213

INTRODUCTION

Mine is a family of five: myself; my wife, Kristine Carole Cano-Jackson; our daughter, Cheyanne Eve; our son, Quinton Stone; and our nephew, Thomas Konrad (TK) Ochoa, who has been living with us since June of 2007.

On June 10, 2009, Quinton, who was nine years old, passed away in the most improbable accident. I mean for this book to share who we were before this awful tragedy. It is written primarily from my perspective, so these pages illustrate just how misguided I was as I intently focused on providing for the family while trying to find meaning in my life. Does this sound familiar to any of you? Our annual vacation in June of 2009 marked a turning point in our lives. Quinton was called home right at the point when I was searching for a sign, searching for a deeper purpose and meaning for my life. When we reviewed the events leading up to the accident, the accident itself, and the mind-blowing events afterward, I realized that the questions I had been asking had been answered.

We hope that you will be able to see through our grief and our loss to see the blessing, the understanding that these events left us with. Some are unable to, and as more time passes, it seems a greater percentage of those we share with hear about our loss and don't want to hear any more; they are essentially stuck in the grief of imagining it happening to them or maybe they think it odd that we speak of Quinton in the present tense.

After you read about the accident, you may wonder, as Kristine and I did, why we survived even though Quinton did not. You see, both of us were hit by an airborne car as we stood outside the passenger side of our vehicle, which was parked thirty feet off the road; we somehow survived while Quinton, who was not hit by the vehicle, died.

As we healed and relived the accident over and over in our minds, we began to realize there is more to our reality. We have come to understand the implications of our experiences and now refer to them as Quinton's messages. We survived to share these messages verbally, through written media, and through the way we live out the rest of our lives. We have been sharing ever since.

The writing of this book, *Quinton's Messages*, was a reliving of a struggle that I only recently became aware of. I have spent a lifetime behind a self-made wall, hiding from my own emotions. When Quinton left us, that didn't change; it was only exacerbated. Within an hour of the accident, I began attempting to manage the emotions of everyone around me as I hid from my own. Yes, I cried more than I remember ever crying, but I am not sure if I have yet grieved.

Within a week of the accident, I pointedly asked not to be left alone; I shared in person, with one or two people at a time, as I began to understand the implications of our shared nightmare. The responses of those I visited with cemented my understanding that within our experiences is a message intended to be shared. By July 2009, I realized that I needed to get in front of a larger audience before the sadness could overwhelm me. I casually mentioned this desire to a couple of my friends, and within two weeks of those conversations, I found myself speaking in front of fifty-five of my friends and peers. This thirty-two-minute session was videotaped and put on the Internet at www.vimeo.com/7314888. It seems a lifetime has passed since then as I sit here and reflect.

Initially, the vast majority of the people we spoke with could see past the obvious sadness, hear the messages, and understand their implications. For others, the vision Quinton has provided of life beyond death is frightening, but we find it comforting—more than comforting to be honest. If I hadn't been blessed with Quinton's visits after he passed away, I am afraid I would have fallen apart.

Quinton's Messages

We are all human and have different perspectives that have been formed by our own life experiences. There isn't a right or a wrong in the terms that most of us think of. Some of those who heard of our loss had nothing to say, as I tended to do when confronted with a friend's loss prior to my own. Others struggled to find words that might provide us with comfort. People are genuinely good, as we saw firsthand, but all one individual could only say was, "That is bad luck." He wanted to say something, didn't know what to say, and that was all he could come up with. That is okay; I appreciate him wanting to say something, but I gently corrected him by telling him "luck had nothing to do with it," nothing to do with it at all.

As we've shared Quinton's messages, we've received amazing messages in return. There is a chapter devoted to the experiences of family, friends, and acquaintances who have also sensed, in some way, their transitioned loved ones. It was at this point in our journey that we really began to understand the scope of what we were dealing with. Maybe it would be better put if I said we began to understand, given the commonality of our shared experiences, that they are the norm and not the exception. With that understanding came the knowledge that we are intended to testify to our experiences.

Several of our friends suggested that I write a book. My response was usually the same, "What? Me, write a book?" I have never written a book in my life, have never even contemplated writing a book, but over a relatively short period of time, I came to realize this book was indeed meant to be written. Acquaintances were pretty receptive, but some would immediately ask if I had written a book before. No was the answer, and they would look at me kind of oddly. No was the answer to the question, but what did that have to do with it? With what we had seen and experienced, whether I had written a book before or not had no bearing on this project.

So here it is.

I hope and pray that you can see beyond our grief as we have and hear the messages that Quinton has left us with.

Chapter One

FOUND AND LOST AGAIN

When I was twenty-seven, a voice sounded crystal clear in my mind. The voice said that I was ready to be a father and that I would be a good father. It got my attention, and it cut through the mindless chatter that usually goes on in my head. The message surprised me with its clarity and timing. I was single and in a great relationship with an older woman who already had two children but couldn't have any more. But the voice was so clear, that I broke it off with her, and Kristine entered my life not long afterward.

At the time, Kristine was working for Honeywell in the accounts payable department. My father, and eventually I, would pick up monthly janitorial contract checks from her. Fearing being laid off, Kristine spoke to my father about looking for work, and at the time, we had an open position in the office. I interviewed her over lunch at a nearby restaurant, but the conversation was awkward; I tried to find some commonality between the two of us, while she was all business, focused entirely on landing a job. We definitely did not hit it off, but I rationalized that I didn't need to hit it off with her for her to be the right person for the job. She had a bubbly personality and was quite attractive with short dark hair, brown eyes, and a curvy physique; she was just distant with me.

Not long after she started, I could tell that she really didn't like me. She must have thought I was a slacker, because I usually came in after she opened the office. I showed up after working out in a local gym and, often, after performing janitorial inspections at our accounts. She also seemed to struggle to understand how I could switch back and forth between my all-business mode and my easygoing mode. Although Kristine and I didn't hit it off, she was a cutie—still is, for that matter—and did a great job in the office for us.

She was engaged to a young man in California when we hired her. Because she was engaged, I made it a point to keep an eye on her and often times stuck my head out of my office when the guys came by and invariably flirted with her to remind them that she was engaged. This went on for about six weeks from the time she started in December of 1991 through the month of January. During this period of time, a mutual attraction was developing, but I tried not to give it a thought, even though I was pretty miserable at being single. Ever perceptive, Kristine clearly noticed this and one day, she asked, "What are you doing this weekend?"

"Nothing," I said.

"Well, my family and I are spending the day at Lake Pleasant this Saturday [February 1, 1992]. Would you like to join us?"

She thought I would decline and was surprised when I accepted. That day is still etched in my mind.

I arrived at the appointed time, which was after they had arrived, settled in, and started cooking breakfast. After parking, I jumped out of my white, four-wheel drive Dodge Ram Charger and walked over to Kristine, who immediately introduced me to her family. The women (Kristine's mother, Nellie, and Kristine's sister, Julie) greeted me with hugs, and Ed, Kristine's father, greeted me with a firm handshake. I was confused; I thought hugs were foreplay, as my immediate family shared very little, if any, of these physical displays. Eventually, I became known for hugs as well, and I am happy to say that I now know they are not foreplay! Their welcoming me into their family was a major crossroad as I began to learn what I was intended to learn.

I couldn't argue with the universe at that point. As Kristine points out in her retelling of that day, "We have been together ever since." What is even more interesting is that we look like family. In pictures of me both as a baby and a boy, I look almost exactly like our nephews on Kristine's side of the family. How does that happen? We look the same, but we do not have the same blood line. Yes. Kristine and I were intended all along to be married. Kristine and her family taught me the meaning of family and the meaning of love.

My parents moved to Las Vegas not long before our wedding, in part because my father knew that he and I could no longer work together. While we both believed in providing superior service, we had different philosophies on how service should be provided and how our employees should be treated. He also knew that I wanted to feel special by taking care of his company for him; his relationships had become my relationships over the years. My father realized that I had grown to manhood and that if I couldn't manage the company the way I believed it should be managed, I would probably resign. Meanwhile, he saw the success we were having and was ready to take a backseat.

The business flourished as I hired a management team that shared my vision of service and integrity. The team I assembled doubled the size of the business, which eventually had over four hundred employees and billed over five million dollars a year. I touched a lot of lives during this period of my life, and on some level, I was just beginning to understand some of the gifts I had been granted from God.

Kristine and I quickly married after she broke it off with her fiancé. To be honest, she had begun to cut her ties to him before she met me, because she didn't want him to abandon his family in California for her in Arizona. I was in a hurry to get married in large part because I didn't want her to discover that I was damaged goods. Yes, I am and was a good guy, but at that point in my life, I had serious issues. I didn't understand love, didn't know how to love, and was too into myself—period. That was part of the reason my first marriage failed. At work, fear of failure motivated me, but at home I was completely self-centered. After we were married, Kristine saw me for what I was (a problem), and we almost didn't make it. While we were on a vacation in Colorado, she decided she was through with me, but upon our return to Arizona we discovered that she was pregnant and decided to try to make it work. Kristine's pregnancy was absolutely horrible. She had hyperemesis, which is morning sickness that lasts all day long for months. She ended up losing twenty-five pounds while on an IV for five months at home. I was no longer quite so self-centered, but I didn't know how to handle that. I was still ignorant, and I saw that I could not fix the problem, so I kept to myself. I didn't understand that I could comfort her and ease her pain. It is a wonder we stayed married.

When Cheyanne was born on May 27, 1993, in Glendale, Arizona, I glimpsed something that I could not remember ever being exposed to: unconditional love. In a sense, I was found. As I watched Cheyanne emerging into the world, I was struck by just how miraculous an event it was. I pondered her beautiful face during birth. She came out of Kristine's birth canal head first and face up. Her eyebrows, nose, and little mouth were perfect. I could not take my eyes off her hands: her fingers were amazing down to the smallest detail; her cuticles and fingernails were perfect. Tears welled up in my eyes as I took in this miracle that happens every day. The obstetrician looked at me with a twinkle in his eye and said, "Now you see why I do what I do." There was a picture taken of me holding Cheyanne when we arrived home. My muscles were flexed as I cradled her, but the look in my face said it all. I loved her unconditionally and would do anything for her.

For six years, I kept it together. I balanced work and my family life just as I expected I could. I kept the two separate, but my family was my priority. Being a good father and a good husband meant more to me than the family business did. While the business excelled, I had plenty for Kristine and Cheyanne when I came home. I awoke early every morning and fed Cheyanne before going to the gym. I treasured our mornings together; after feeding her, I would put her in bed with Kristine. As Cheyanne grew older and began to crawl, sometimes I would sit at my desk in the mornings. She would climb out of her carrier and roam across the top of the desk, eventually coming to the computer keyboard to pound on the keys. I would laugh at her, and we always had a grand time.

Quinton's Messages

After spending twelve years in Phoenix, Arizona (starting in May of 1986), I desperately wanted to move back to Colorado, where I had spent my formative years, but Kristine didn't share my enthusiasm. Her immediate family lived in Phoenix, and much of her extended family lived in California. Meanwhile, competition with a national janitorial firm in Phoenix was becoming tougher, and our profit margins were shrinking. By the time I hired a professional accountant to help me restructure the salaries my parents were earning, our operating cash was all but gone. We lost a major contract to a national bid that represented a fifteen-year relationship, because we only provided service in the state of Arizona.

Shortly thereafter, when I was thirty-four years old, I sold the business to the same janitorial company that had been giving us fits. My father, who was stoned on prescription pills at the time, never understood the details of the deal. I paid off the lines of credit and left my parents with a nice pile of cash that my dad proceeded to blow over the coming years. I had arranged to be transferred to Colorado to take over the Colorado branch of the firm that had purchased ours. Knowing my father well enough by that point in my life (meaning that, if he had his druthers, he would probably not give me a dime), I wired fifty-nine thousand dollars directly to the title company on the home we purchased. Even though I was entitled to much more, that was what I took from the deal. I wanted to leave my parents in great financial shape, and I did what I intended to do, not that my father was pleased by my efforts.

We arrived in Conifer on September 8, 1998, and settled in. Kristine put on a happy face, but she desperately missed her family. Even though she made friends quickly, living so far from home was a struggle for her.

It was at this point that my struggles returned. Away from the family umbrella, out in the world, I began to define myself once again by my job and my performance on the job, all the while becoming less involved as a husband and father. As this condition worsened over the years, it evolved to the point that, oftentimes, when I was physically there with my family, I wasn't mentally present. I would be preoccupied with work or just plain mentally exhausted and wishing to just quietly sit somewhere with no responsibilities. Increasingly, I was losing myself and not enjoying the moment. I viewed my stint with the national janitorial firm as a failure, because I hadn't been able to turn around a branch that had been losing money for years. After less than six months as the branch manager, I knew I had failed, because we were still losing money. They felt the same way and were prepared to terminate my employment, but a funny thing happened. My employer floated a trial balloon with our largest client by telling them of their plans to terminate my employment, and our client told them that, if they did, they would lose the contract. I ended up in sales, and much to my surprise, I had some success.

Meanwhile, we had a new addition to the family. Quinton was born on December 15, 1999, at 9:37 in the evening at Swedish Medical Hospital in Denver, Colorado. His coming was a miracle in the sense that he was totally unexpected. After Kristine's very difficult pregnancy with Cheyanne and two miscarriages afterward, we didn't expect to have another child. We had been told that we had been lucky to have Cheyanne.

Because of those difficulties, when Kristine wasn't feeling well in March of 1999, we hadn't a clue that she might be pregnant. After we showed up in the doctor's office and had an examination, the doctor came out with something of a mixed expression and let Kristine know she was pregnant. The moment was kind of comical, because the doctor didn't know if this would be a happy occasion for us or if being pregnant wouldn't be received well. She asked, "Well, did you want to be pregnant?"

Quinton's timing could not have been better. All of us were equally excited about the addition to our family, especially Cheyanne, who had previously expressed the desire for a sibling. At six years old, Cheyanne was so brave and responsible in how she helped to care for Kristine during the pregnancy. Kristine's pregnancy with Quinton was almost as bad as it had been with Cheyanne. This time, she only lost fifteen pounds. Cheyanne would come home from school and make Kristine Top Ramen noodles.

His arrival changed everything. He came out with fair complexion, brown eyes, and a full head of dark brown hair. It was almost scary how much hair he had. He appeared to have a cone head, which left me momentarily frightened, but we soon realized that everything was normal. Quinton was always a happy baby and almost as happy as Cheyanne had been as a baby. Our family was complete. Cheyanne and Quinton got along great. For that matter, all of us did, but it seemed like I was always working. No more so than most of you reading this book, but I wished I could spend more time with my family.

Despite a measure of success at work, I knew that I could not stay long-term, because the company was having difficulty servicing some of the business I had brought in, and I knew my reputation would be tarnished by their failure. I had always aspired to be a property manager of commercial office buildings, because I had always looked up to the managers I had worked for. My opportunity came in the fall of 2000, and I made the jump.

My people skills and ability to provide service are transferrable to most fields, but it was initially a struggle to mold myself into a corporate being. I tended to be a little too loose with my comments and behavior for a corporate job. Even though I tried desperately to tone down my comments and jokes, I still managed to get myself into quite the predicament during my first year of employment in my new field. Just one flip comment was enough. As my asset manager told me, a hundred atta-boys can be overshadowed by one "Oh shit." Indeed! That lesson was learned and internalized over time. I would interact with tenants and vendors in my usual gregarious way but keep my head down in my office and just do my job. Eventually, I found success while learning the ins and outs of property management, but all the while I was beginning to realize that something was missing.

My ship came in, or so I thought, on the wings of a promotion from assistant general manager to general manager in the spring of 2007. After several years of staying out of trouble and performing well, I was still surprised on some level. I had been looking for some time for a growth opportunity outside the company. When it came within the company, it caught me unprepared. When my boss told me that he and the asset manager needed to talk to me, I immediately said, with a smile, "Well, I know I haven't messed up, so what's up?" He smiled back and indicated that I hadn't messed up.

Over the course of the next fifteen months, my salary increased 33 percent as I improved the curb appeal of my new assignment while minimizing the operating budget increases and getting to know the tenants. It was a dream job that came with a wonderful staff intact. All I had to do was show up, treat people the way I would like to be treated, address what I thought were deficiencies, and communicate. There were some new levels of reporting that I had to master, but after lowering my heart rate, I muddled through and was again surprised that my asset manager was pleased with the results.

As I marveled at this success, I became aware of a new theme in my conversations with those closest to me. I eventually became aware that I had been complaining about it for some time. At least four times a year, I would complain, "We are worshiping a false God; we are worshiping the almighty dollar bill. We have lost our spirituality." Over and over, this theme crept into my conversations, but I couldn't figure out what to do about it. On some level, while I said "we," I realized that I was referring to myself.

My last new job, in 2008, took me to a salary that I never thought I would earn and knew I didn't deserve. I made the change anyway and was miserable. I jumped into the new position with gusto as I employed all the knowledge gained over the years to make the asset more efficient and environmentally friendly while dealing with floods and compressor failures. It didn't take me long to realize I had made a mistake and was in a no-win scenario. I hung on into 2009 just to prove to myself that I could endure the nightmare.

That was the place I found myself when we left for vacation in June 2009. I knew I had sold out; I knew that I was worshiping a false God (that being money); I knew I was lost; and I was consciously looking for the light. I knew I had lost myself, and I was at the point of walking through the rest of my life and living through my children.

In short, I thought my life was over, and I was fine with that.

Chapter Two

QUINTON STONE JACKSON

Our son, an angel and our blessing, came to us three days after my thirty-fifth birthday. We took Kristine down to Swedish Memorial Hospital in the morning, and the nurses asked if she wanted an epidural. Kristine's eyes lit up; this was a significant change from when Cheyanne had been born in Phoenix six and a half years earlier, when the epidural wasn't administered until the pain was unbearable. After Kristine responded with an enthusiastic yes to the nurses, the epidural was administered, and we settled in for a long wait. Nellie, Kristine's mother, was there with me in Kristine's hospital room, but we had left Cheyanne with a close friend and neighbor, Sally Lapham, who had befriended us when we had arrived in Conifer a short fifteen months earlier.

With Kristine quietly sleeping, Nellie and I looked at each other and decided we should go downstairs to the bookstore. I picked up a five hundred–page work of fiction about the New Madrid seismic fault located in the eastern part of this country. About the time I finished the book some twelve hours later, Quinton was ready to make his arrival.

Quinton's name was originally going to be Quinton Coal Jackson; we had decided on his name five months before. But Kristine went into early labor with kidney stones in October, three months early. When that happened, we rushed Kristine to the hospital, where they admitted her and then stabilized her. On the morning they had scheduled surgery to remove the kidney stones she passed them and was allowed to come home. At this point, we decided on Quinton Stone Jackson.

Ernie Jackson

The nurse came in shortly after 9:00 p.m. to check on Kristine. Immediately the nurse's eyes opened wide. She pronounced it was time and rushed to get the delivery team in place. After just a few minutes of pushing, Kristine held Quinton in her arms. We were released the next day.

All of us spent a lot of time holding and cuddling with Quinton. I kept the wood stove blazing hot, so our home 8,900 feet above sea level was toasty warm. When I wasn't working, I was always cuddling with and kissing Quinton; for this, I have to thank Cheyanne. Having a little girl first was just what I needed. After cuddling with and kissing her for years, it only seemed natural to do the same with Quinton. Otherwise, I am afraid that, when he was born, I would have given him a football uniform, so to speak, and tried to toughen him up.

Ed and Nellie Cano were there with us when Quinton was born, and they visited us often, or we would visit them in Arizona, preferably during the winter. They were fixtures in Quinton's life. They would often comment as they looked at Quinton that he was an old soul, meaning that his maturity level and the look in his eyes left them with the impression that he was older than his years.

During the summer, I often stayed in Colorado while my family visited Ed and Nellie for weeks at a time. At that point in my life, I was fully immersed in the grand illusion perpetrated by our society. I worked for a publicly owned national janitorial company after Quinton was born and as a commercial property manager during the majority of his life. I realize now that I worked more to find meaning in my life and define who I was rather than just to put food on the table. Oh, how misguided I was, as so many of us are.

It wasn't until much later in life that I began to realize how old Quinton's soul was, and not until after he was called home did I begin to understand the implications of that simple statement. So many of us comment on old souls and old eyes; those statements imply that we have lived here before, maybe several times. As our society becomes more spiritual, more and more are coming to believe in reincarnation. Comments about "old souls" or "old eyes" speak to the possibility of reincarnation, whether we believe in it or not.

Quinton absolutely hated the cold weather during the first five years of his life. He spent much of the Colorado winters sick with all sorts of colds, but when he felt well, all he wanted was to be outside. Once, when he was about two years old, Kristine and Cheyanne took him sledding with some friends of the family at Meyer's Ranch, a nearby hill the community used for sledding and tubing. I stayed home recovering from yet another tiring week of work. While I was warm and at home, the phone rang. Kristine was calling, asking me to pick up Quinton, who was freezing. When I arrived not long after her call, I found Quinton in tears. After a short drive home, I cuddled with him until he was warm and happy yet again.

As he grew older, his tolerance for the cold weather improved, but he still indicated that he wanted to live in Arizona with Nellie when he was older. As you get to know Quinton a little bit better, you may have a greater appreciation of that statement.

When Kristine and I reminisce, we recall that, although Quinton hated being cold in his early years, as he grew and when he wasn't sick, he did spend time playing in the snow. While using our snowblower to remove thirteen inches of snow one February morning in 2011, I had a recollection of Quinton walking beside the snowblower when he was still with us, in step with me as he wore his navy-blue snowsuit and a hood to protect his head from the cold. He did this so that, as the snow left the chute, it would immediately cascade all over him. Quinton was probably seven or eight years old at the time, and he loved doing this for some reason I never understood. I wouldn't let him do it if the snow was wet and heavy because I worried that it would hurt him. In this memory, I smiled as I watched him laugh and giggle within the waterfall of snow before I finally said, "All right, Quinton, that is enough. I don't want you to get hurt."

He looked at me as if to plead for a little more before saying, "Come on, Dad, just a little while longer?"

"No, son, the snow blower could pick up a rock or pine cone and throw it at you and hurt you."

He gave me a kind of exasperated look before he obeyed. I was forever cautious as I tried to protect my son.

Kids in the snow Apr 2005

Quinton's Messages

Almost every winter we received a lot of snow—anywhere from eight feet to nineteen feet during the entire snow season that began in September some years and lasted until June. During the winter, the snow piled up five or six feet deep alongside the driveway. As Quinton grew older, like so many boys his age, he endeavored to make snow forts; with the many piles of deep snow, he and the children of the Linehan family, our immediate neighbors to the south, had ample opportunity. The Linehan family members were dear friends. The parents, George and Mary, had seven children: Patrick, Brendan, Bryan, Katie, Thomas, Sean, and Aiden. The youngest were Quinton's best friends. In 2009, Thomas was ten, Sean was six, and Aiden was three. They built their forts and tunnels under the snow while our male Puggle, Odie, played alongside them.

Even though it seemed I was always at work, I didn't often miss an opportunity to admonish Quinton about the risks associated with tunneling in the snow—you know, trying to keep him safe. Our family tried—and mostly succeeded in—keeping scary stuff away from Quinton. Still though, after Quinton passed away, I learned of his close call while tunneling. One day while Kristine was inside and I was at work, Quinton said, "Mom, a snow tunnel fell on me, but Odie pulled me out."

Kristine responded with fear and relief as she said, "Remember what Dad said about tunneling in the snow, son? Please be careful in the future."

We dodged a bullet there.

During the winter of 2007, we had one bad scare. Quinton was sick and really having a tough time breathing. Kristine took him to the doctor in Conifer who, after realizing how low Quinton's blood oxygen levels were, called for an ambulance. Kristine called me, and I left the office immediately. I met them at Children's Hospital off of I-225. Quinton was on a respirator, and the hospital staff administered steroids and antihistamines to treat his nearly closed bronchial passages. All of us were frightened, including Quinton, who was very quiet while this was going on. He just sat and looked at us with sad eyes as we tried to look confident. We were concerned that Quinton might die, and the thought terrified us. Quinton watched us, and I am sure he saw the fear in our eyes. There it was: death peeking in at us. It was a precursor of things to come.

Right after Quinton was born, we purchased a hot tub, built a foundation, and placed it on the north side of our home. As the years passed, Quinton and I would often be the only ones using it during the winter. Kristine and, in some respect, Cheyanne avoided the hot tub during the winter months; they rationalized that it was too cold to use. No matter what I said about the hot tub being designed for winter use, they were still reluctant. They preferred using the hot tub during the summer. On weekends when I could reconnect with my family a little bit, before or after making fried potatoes for breakfast, Quinton and I spent time in the hot tub. Those moments were always special to me; my son and I were together a lot when I was home. During the winter, icicles would form on the hot tub cover, and as soon as I opened the hot tub and helped Quinton get in if he needed help, he made a beeline for the icicles with an intent look. He would break an icicle off, smiling, sit in the steamy water, and eat it until there was nothing left. Then he stood up and reached for another. Smiling as I watched, I asked, "Are you enjoying that?" as I broke off one for myself. Quinton always smiled back and answer yes while nodding in the affirmative. When he finished the last one, he would only be sad for a moment and then become absorbed by huge icicles hanging off the house or by a bird or a plane in the sky.

Moving the snow that fell during the winter seemed like a full-time task for me. Somewhere in the back of my mind, I realized I didn't have to be so anal about clearing the driveway and piling the snow just to achieve the largest piles possible; somewhere in the back of my mind, I realized that the snow would eventually melt of its own accord thanks to the spring sun, but I still shoveled. The property manager in me reasoned that I was mitigating risk by reducing the chance that someone would slip and fall while visiting us. On a deeper level, I was simply trying to make myself feel okay or worthy. When the snow did begin melting, I would create channels for the water to more easily run downhill and to avoid puddles.

One day, when Quinton was probably seven years old, I looked out the window and saw him doing the very same thing while wearing faded blue jeans and a lightweight red jacket, and with his brown hair blowing in the spring breeze. Yes, he played in the puddles as he created channels, or he made a dam in the channel and jump in the puddle he created and then open the channel up for the water to drain. Quinton did that a lot. Naturally, I assumed, this was a learned behavior from watching me do it so often, but still I wondered. He would do so with such intent and focus that, sometimes, I wondered if maybe he wasn't simply mimicking my behavior but was doing it because he enjoyed doing it.

Regarding the snow, there was one thing that I did have to do on occasion: shovel the north-facing roof. The snow would pile up, and that invariably resulted in an ice dam forming at the edge. Quinton was never allowed on the roof of our home, but during one winter of heavy snowfall, his friend Thomas, who was fourteen months older, and he climbed up onto the roof of a shed I built during the summer of 2006. The snow was so deep around the shed after I shoveled the roof that they were able to simply half climb, half crawl up the snow to its roof. I guess they called it cleaning the snow off the shed roof, but it looked an awful lot like having a blast. I didn't have to worry much about them getting hurt doing so either, because the snow was so deep.

My son was my partner. While I am not sure of others' family dynamics, our family seemed to have two camps: oftentimes, it was the boys and the girls. Kristine and Cheyanne were like-minded; Quinton and I were also like-minded. I don't know if anything illustrated this more than a story about a cat we had. This cat was a male named Cougar who, like so many we have had over the years, sometimes didn't like using the litter box. This kind of thing drove me mad. I worked so hard to provide a nice home only to have a pet make messes. Kristine and

Cheyanne didn't seem to mind. They would clean up the messes while agreeing not to tell me, which became a common theme in our home—"Don't tell Dad." One day, I was walking around our home when I caught a whiff of urine coming from our couch. If you knew me, it would not surprise you to see me with my nose to the couch looking for the spot. I found it with a flair of distaste and immediately went to Kristine. She played it off.

"No, what are talking about?" she asked. "The cat didn't pee on the couch."

She almost had me believing that I was mistaken, but Quinton, who was probably about four at the time, came to me after she was out of earshot and told me that the cat had indeed peed on our couch, and then he showed me the spot. I was so proud of my son. He wasn't going to lie; he told the truth. I remember hamming it up for several weeks by saying that Quinton and I were on the good team and the others were on the bad team. I probably went a little overboard with the good team/bad team bit, but I love him so.

That summer of 2004 when he was four and a half years old, he asked several times for me to remove the training wheels from his bike and teach him how to ride it. He didn't nag, mind you; he seemed to make his request a couple of times a month, and I would always say that, yes, I would do so. Still being misguided and lost in my routine of working at my job and working around the house for the purpose of finding inner worthiness, I didn't make time for this simple task in a quick enough manner. As only Quinton could, he became a little exasperated with his dad.

One day, he said, "Dad, if I pay you, will you take my training wheels off and teach me how to ride my bike?"

I was dumbfounded, amused, and ashamed all at once. At all of four years old, Quinton was struggling to get through to me and wanted it badly enough to offer to pay me. He sliced right through my issues and got my attention. I remember being amazed by Quinton as I slowly took off the training wheels and watched. He jumped on the bike seat and put his feet on the pedals as I held his bike. I guided him around in a large circle as he got his balance. Within five minutes, he was riding without my help and would not again need my help riding a bike. I really didn't think he was ready to let go of the training wheels, but he showed me.

Bike riding became something of a tradition with our family and we had many more traditions, another one was our breakfast. This tradition was initially more of a personal tradition that became our tradition when Kristine and I married: fried potatoes and eggs for breakfast at least one weekend morning during the month. I don't cook much, but I have always made fried potatoes for breakfast (and fried chicken for dinner on occasion). When it came to breakfast, coffee was first. Ever observant, Quinton watched as I made mine with creamer in a bottle. At some point in time, Quinton asked me for some coffee after having a taste of mine. I love my son, so that I wouldn't dare give him the regular stuff and I didn't want to give him too much caffeine, so I created a concoction of milk, coffee, creamer, and sugar. It was lighter on the caffeine but heavy on the sweetness. Anything that tasted good I would say had extra love. Yeah, I know; health nuts are cringing right now, but this was how we rolled! Quinton asked for his special coffee whenever I made breakfast. This must have started about the time he was four or five years old. On a couple of occasions, he asked Kristine to make him some coffee, but he wasn't satisfied with her coffee; it just plain didn't have enough love mixed in. Hmmm, maybe I wasn't such a good father after all, I think as I sit here recalling the memories with a big smile on my face.

For much of Quinton's young life, he was either in my arms or right next to me. We just wanted to be together when I wasn't working. The pictures taken over the years illustrate just how close we were, but it is in more than pictures. As bad as my memory can be, I remember our times together—cuddling together watching cartoons or some action show with fast cars, walking through the woods, or whatever. He was my little buddy.

Quinton took after me by being an early riser. Typically, I was up between five and six in the morning during the week for work, but even on the weekends, I rarely slept past seven. Quinton would be there with me. Oftentimes, we sat together side by side and cuddle if it was cold. Or he sat next to me as I read the paper and drank coffee. Sometimes, we talked about whatever he wanted to talk about. Sometimes, he would share something from one of the cartoons he watched on Cartoon Network, like *Star Wars*, or I might point something out in the newspaper that I thought he might find interesting. Other times, we just simply sat together in relative silence. Just to be near one another was good. I long for those moments now.

Kristine was almost always the one to help both the kids with their homework. I would help on occasion, but Cheyanne especially didn't enjoy my help because I usually only gave hints in an effort to help her figure it out herself. With Quinton, it was no different. Unfortunately, most of the time, I was too tired to help consistently and to do so with good energy, so Kristine did it. Quinton struggled with reading, and he did well with math, but at times, he would be too tired to focus.

During what must have been the spring of 2009, Quinton sat at the table, unable to focus on his math homework. It was easy stuff for him, but he wanted help. As I looked at his work, I shared with him what my boss had shared with me. I told him to take a step back and look at the work from a different perspective. We called it the sniff test.

Quinton's Messages

"Quinton," I told him, "take a look at your answer and the problem, and see if it makes sense." I shared that if, after taking a step back and looking at the problem logically, it didn't make sense, then it must be dodo. I sniffed and said, "That smells like dodo," while looking at a problem that he knew he had done wrong. We laughed as he looked at me like I had lost my mind. Typically, when I helped them with their homework laughter wasn't the result, so this was a special moment, and I think it stuck with him because he would always smile that sweet Quinton smile with humor in his eyes when I referred to the sniff test.

One morning after he had grown up, I could not sleep and was working on the computer at four o'clock. Quinton woke up to relieve himself and then came downstairs to me to check on me. This was probably in 2009 before our last vacation together. As he walked part of the way down the stairs, his sleepy eyes registering concern as he asked, "Are you okay, Dad?" This was yet another special moment, as so many moments with Quinton were special. He was genuinely concerned about me. In hindsight, I think he knew on some level that something was wrong; maybe he knew I was hurting inside as I struggled to know my purpose and ultimately find a level of peace.

Some of our most enjoyable moments came in the car. Quinton almost always rode with me. Often, the family would have to divide and conquer, which resulted in Cheyanne going with Kristine and Quinton going with me. Other times, Quinton and I would just be together in the car to go see a movie or run errands. I had a 1998 SS Camaro from 2000 to 2006. This vehicle had a hatch in the back. When Quinton was two and three years old, he loved to lie in the back of the vehicle on the hatch and stare out the window as I drove. Yes, I know, that was bad form on my part, but it made him happy. Getting into an accident and losing my son wasn't even a concern or a thought. I was firmly entrenched within the illusion of control so many of us have in the western cultures. I believed that I could protect my son no matter the circumstance—silly me and silly us. Yes, I know, this is just one example of putting Quinton and me into harm's way. Nothing happened, but I would eventually learn that I was not in control.

Another car memory was of me singing, invariably at the top of my lungs and poorly. Both Cheyanne and Quinton had to endure my singing. Cheyanne often looked around, hoping nobody she knew was in another car nearby. With Quinton, it wasn't much different, but he seemed to have an affinity with the classic rock I loved. He gave me the impression of enjoying it as much as I did and one song in particular: "Radar Love" by Golden Earring. I don't know if it was the bass guitar rift or what, but he really liked that song, and it always came on the radio when we were driving. I turned it up every time and, sang along with the song, and encourage Quinton to sing with me, though I don't recall him ever doing it.

As we grew older, Quinton became very cautious, and I did as well. Quite possibly, that was because of a rather traumatic accident that we experienced when I was driving one weekend in the spring of 2006. I was tired and enjoying my time at home. Kristine and Cheyanne wanted to go shopping in town, but it was snowing, so they asked me to drive them. In this circumstance, I would usually just say no, complain that I was too tired, and say, "I go to town five days a week and have no intention of driving to town on the weekend." This time was different. I didn't want to disappoint them yet again, so I said sure, and we were off. We made it to the mall without incident, and I didn't even complain. They shopped a bit while Quinton and I went to RadioShack to look at remote-control cars.

The road was very slushy on the way home, and I was overconfident. We were driving Kristine's Suzuki XL-7. A tow truck passed us and splashed us with slush, which annoyed me. After putting the Suzuki in four-wheel drive, I pulled out of the slow lane and hit the gas. All four tires spun, and we began to fishtail. I wasn't concerned, because I had done this hundreds of times, but not in Kristine's vehicle. I never let off the gas as I straightened the car out. All of a sudden, we spun over one hundred degrees to the left and were heading to the grass median separating the two lanes of Highway 285. It was in slow motion—what a cliché, but it was. In my mind's eye I saw that we would slide into the median and then into oncoming traffic. *This is going to be very, very bad,* I thought, *maybe fatal.* None of us screamed or said anything as we slid sideways into the median. It all happened too quickly. But a stout road sign stopped us in our tracks. We went from moving too quickly for the conditions to a dead stop in an instant. The whole passenger side of the car was creased by the road sign. When we hit the sign, our vehicle began to tip over onto its side. We were briefly on two wheels. Then the sign that had stopped our forward motion also prevented us from rolling, and we crashed back down to the ground with such force that the driver's side front tire blew out. Somehow nobody was hurt. Kristine and Cheyanne were on the passenger side of the vehicle. Either one of them could have been killed or seriously hurt, but somehow we took the impact of the sign right where the front door and rear passenger door met. It blew out both of their windows.

It was snowing hard as we looked at each other, with me feeling really stupid and lucky at the same time. The girls were happy to be unhurt and very, very angry with me. Quinton, who was sitting directly behind me, didn't say too much if anything at all. Instead of waiting for help, I slipped the vehicle back into park, restarted it, and drove out of the median. We drove another mile or so and pulled into a small office park so I could change the tire, and an interesting thing happened. The moment I stepped outside of the vehicle, it stopped snowing as if on cue. I thought that odd; I was prepared to get soaked. I finished changing the tire quickly, and as I climbed back into the vehicle, it started snowing just as hard as it had been previously.

As we drove away, I cracked jokes to try to lighten the girls' spirits. I commented that we had an angel watching over us. Their moods didn't change; they were mad at me for several days, and I just now understand the significance of the whole event. It wasn't our time, and we weren't alone. Our guardian angels were there protecting us. Hmmm, maybe we are never alone.

It is very interesting that Quinton was called home while we were being extra careful and not as the result of my recklessness. This must be part of the message, that being *the shattering of the proverbial illusion of control*. If I could find a way to claim responsibility for my son's transition, I would not have been able to get the messages myself. If Quinton or any of my family had died as a result of my stupidity in the spring of 2006, I would have been destroyed by the knowledge that I was the cause.

Truth be told, I might not have gotten the message anyway if Quinton's first contact hadn't occurred so quickly.

Quinton wasn't just here for me. He was always there for Kristine and actually took care of Cheyanne when Kristine and I had an occasional date night. That's right; that statement wasn't a mistake or typo. Although Quinton was six and a half years younger than Cheyanne, when they were alone and it was dark outside, Quinton comforted Cheyanne and made sure she was okay. They spent the time together watching TV, typically a scary movie, and eating popcorn or ramen noodles with extra Louisiana hot sauce. Quinton was always the first to greet Kristine when she came home from her part-time job as an office manager in an Evergreen chiropractic office. Kristine had one late night a week, and Quinton would always greet her with a smile and a hug as she came up the stairs.

The bond that Kristine and Quinton had was just as special as, if not more special than, my bond with Quinton. He was Kristine's godsend; he brightened her life. It was more than just timing. He was with her during the day while Cheyanne was at school and I was at work. Mornings were their special time. That didn't change once he started school, because he had a later start time than Cheyanne, who was in middle school when Quinton started elementary school. He always greeted Kristine with a smile in the morning when he came into her room and climbed into bed with her to cuddle. All of us will miss Quinton's physical presence for the rest of our lives.

Quinton always helped Kristine around the house. He helped her with laundry and would often be by her side while she cooked dinner, asking questions and, on occasion, actually helping with the meal. Kristine appreciated the fact that she didn't have to ask Quinton more than once to do something, whether that was clearing the table after dinner, putting the dishes in the dishwasher, putting the dishes away, or cleaning his room. There was no back talk or attitude; just love.

Quinton's Messages

Quinton and I spent a lot of time outside together, because both of us enjoy nature. I was forever trying to tidy up our one-acre lot by picking up rocks and pine cones and cutting down dead trees killed by the pine beetle. Quinton was typically there with me, but that began to change as he grew older. He still helped me or came with me, but only if the boys next door weren't available. Our activities changed as well. As Quinton grew, there was less and less to do in the yard, and we spent more time playing catch with the baseball and football. We shot baskets too.

He took after me with a football. I have always enjoyed throwing the football; I played quarterback in high school and for part of a short college career. Quinton's spiral was amazing. While he didn't have any aspirations to play professional sports, he did want to play in the local youth football league. We were reluctant to enroll him, because we were concerned that he might have a bad experience with a coach more intent on winning than helping boys learn the game and how the game invariably helped teach life lessons. The irony is that now I am an assistant high school football coach at my alma mater, Evergreen High School, and am part of a staff that lifts young men up, instead of tearing them down, and all because of Quinton.

As he grew, Quinton got to the point that he went out and shot baskets by himself or with his friends just as I had done when I was his age. Words are inadequate to express how much I miss spending time with him—catch, walks, just being together—marveling at his spirit, his intuitiveness, his light. My son gone; why?

Quinton lived for summer. As soon as the weather warmed, even before all of the snow melted, he and his friends were outside. During most of his life, his best friends were Thomas, Sean, and eventually Aiden Linehan. They played together for hours on end. Often Quinton would make up games, rules and all. All through the summer, all of them would jump on the trampoline, explore the forest, and ride their bikes until they were called home for dinner. That could be an adventure too, because they were usually so focused on their playing that Quinton would not hear us yelling his name at the top of our lungs.

Oh, these fond memories make me smile.

After Quinton transitioned, one of the older Linehan boys, Brendan, shared that when Quinton was still with us, he came over to their home one day to see if the younger boys could play, but they weren't home, so he asked if Brendan could come out and play. I find this amazing. Quinton just wanted to play, and the fact that Brendan was seven years older than him and more interested in spending time with Cheyanne did not matter one bit to him. You might find it even more amazing to know that Brendan, who was sixteen years old at the time, did come out and play with Quinton; they went over and jumped on the trampoline! That was our son; he brought out the best in all of us.

As Quinton continued to grow older and in the last year that he was with us in the physical realm, I gave him more freedom and responsibility. One day, I was cutting down a dead pine tree, and I asked Quinton if he wanted to try the chain saw. He was so excited and His eyes lit up at the prospect of the new experience! I handed the chain saw to him and hovered as he cut the fallen log. When Quinton turned nine years old, he became foreman of the fire pit in our backyard. Once the fire was going, he was responsible for putting just the right amount of wood in to keep the fire going without having it flare up. He understood the seriousness of this responsibility and always did a admirable job.

Quinton's Messages

Not long before we left for vacation, we lost the top of one of our pine trees in a wind storm. The half of the remaining tree sat there with no chance of surviving. Quinton came to me and asked if he could hit what was left of the tree with a stick he had. He really loved sticks of all shapes and sizes—he had a collection—and he carved some with a pocket knife, and he just played with others. I watched him as he started swinging hard at the tree. When I came back to the window only a few minutes later, I was amazed to see that he had stripped the bark off the tree where he had been hitting it.

Typically, I would have found a reason to be stressed about the trees or fire pit, but in his last year I just let him be; I think on some level, I knew he would be leaving us in the near future.

Within the family, I am a known tree-hugger. I have always walked around the yard of our homes over the years and monitored the tree growth. I did it when we moved to Conifer when I was twelve years old, in Phoenix as I patiently tried to create shade, and once again upon my return to Conifer. Late in May of 2009, the young trees in our yard were all showing new growth. Quinton and I walked together, and I excitedly showed him the new growth and asked him not to touch the new sprouts.

"Son, make sure you and your friends don't snap the new growth off the top of the trees. If you do, the tree will have to make a new top."

He looked back at me and said, "Okay, Dad."

The same day, I watched as he explained that to Thomas and Sean.

While walking along the driveway not long before our final vacation together, Quinton and I found a baby pine tree that was not more than two inches tall. I was excited that a new tree had survived that close to the driveway, and Quinton shared my enthusiasm. His enthusiasm was genuine and not that of a child who thinks his parent has lost his mind. Not three feet from where we noticed this baby pine, I found another even smaller baby pine tree after Quinton passed away. I was amazed when I noticed this additional tree during the summer of 2009 and immediately wondered if it was a sign from Quinton.

Late the same month (May 2009), I came home stressed out about work, which was fairly normal at the time. As opposed to sharing my stressed-out state of mind with my family, I typically sat downstairs by myself and tried to unwind by watching the idiot box. On that particular night, I sat watching a rerun of *Star Trek: The Next Generation,* and Quinton came down to sit with me when the episode was halfway through. He sat down on the couch next to me.

"Hey, Dad. How are you?" he asked.

I smiled and said, "I'm fine son," and I was. I was happy he was there with me. There was something unusual about our time together that evening, and it sticks with me to this day. I think he knowingly came downstairs to lift my spirits. Together we sat and watched the episode in which Data made his own child, who was an android like him but had the ability to feel emotions. The fact that Data's android son felt emotion drew interest from Star Fleet, but before Star Fleet could take Data's child to study, the child died. It is rather poignant that we watched that episode together. I don't recall what we said as we watched that sad scene play out, but Quinton's presence that night was profound, as we together watched a program about a father losing his son to death. As the program ended, we watched the credits together and saw that the episode had been made in 1992.

"This episode was made before you were born." After pausing briefly and looking up as I thought about it, I said, "Wow, this episode was made before Cheyanne was born too." Moments like this cut through the everyday routine to get up, go to work, come home, and go to sleep.

Even though I was oblivious to much that was going on around me, I knew that Quinton had a special soul, a special spirit, and I was always concerned that our society would eventually try to dull his bright, shining light. There was one time in particular when I voiced my concern at his school. Quinton was good in math, but he struggled in reading. He ended up taking part in a remedial reading class to get extra attention so he could catch up. Kristine and I sat with the principal of Marshdale Elementary, his teacher, and two young assistants who would be administering the lessons. I pointedly told them that I would not tolerate anything that harmed his spirit in any way. The program was designed to lovingly bring children up to speed, so my worry was not necessary, but I still voiced my concern for Quinton's gentle and loving soul.

Just before our last vacation, near the end of spring of 2009, Kristine persuaded me to be a parent volunteer at the school's Indian Culture Day. I was reluctant, because I was stressed out about work, but I went and was glad that I did. Quinton was very happy that I was there, as was I.

While helping out with some of the events and enjoying being outside among the pine trees, I watched Quinton and some small deer in the area. All of the kids selected Indian names, including Quinton, but the name Quinton selected seemed small in some way, so I made up one that I thought might be more appropriate. I loudly called him He Who Flies Like an Eagle; he cringed and clearly indicated that he wished I stayed quiet.

At the end of the day, we cleaned up and gathered for a closing ceremony. All of us—students, teachers, and parents—stood in a large circle. Several kids were selected to ride broom horses inside the circle. When their time was up after about a minute or so, they would pick people standing in the circle to switch places with them. This went on for quite a while, and many of the children and parents tried to become invisible. Sure enough, one of the teachers who had finished her ride came over to me and away I went, around and around on my broom horse. I hadn't bargained for it, but I rode with vigor, because I was trying to be a good example for Quinton, who rode too. We eventually ended up back in the classroom with about an hour left in the school day.

As I prepared to leave, Quinton asked me to stay and began crying when I rose to leave. I had something to do—wash a vehicle or do some yard work or some other meaningless task. Needless to say, I wish I had stayed. I don't have many regrets, because we did spend a lot of time together, but moments such as that one haunt me. I wish I had stayed.

Ernie Jackson

Chapter Three

OUR VACATIONS: RESPITES FROM THE AGONY

Puerto Penasco, Mexico (a.k.a. Rocky Point), occupies a special place in our hearts and has done so for many years. Ed and Nellie, Kristine's parents, first went there in September 1989 not long after they moved to Phoenix from Whittier, California. Ed immediately fell in love with the old fishing port turned vacation resort on the Sea of Cortez. I was introduced to Rocky Point in the fall of 1990 with a group of acquaintances I knew from Arizona State University.

As I was working on this book on June 8, 2010, we were at Rocky Point on another of our annual trips. There is something about that place, and I really don't quite know what it is. It makes me want to speak Spanish. The waves crashing on the beach soothe my soul while mesmerizing me. The waves also invariably leave me feeling small, like an ant on a sidewalk. Maybe these very waves remind me of a previous life. As always, there is something about sitting in the sun and being outside in the sun that also soothes my soul, no matter the location. There is something about this place that is a beacon for a fresh start, a new beginning or yet another chance to leave the illusion behind and celebrate what is real.

It seems that we have vacationed there with Ed and Nellie once or twice a year since Kristine and I married on April 18, 1992. The visits sometimes included Kristine's sister, Julie, and her husband, Tom Ochoa; on one other occasion, a friend of mine from Evergreen High

School, Bill Coleman and his wife, Tina, came down with us. Back then, Rocky Point was not quite as commercial as it is now, and consequently, there were no rules. People could ride ATVs anywhere along the beach and surrounding sand dunes or drive their vehicles along the beach. Anything went, and often, vehicles buried in the sand were ruined by the incoming tide, and occasionally, we heard of someone being run over by an ATV. None of these events happened while we visited, but we drove our lifted 1993 GMC Suburban up and down the beaches along with the rest.

On one trip with several extended family members, Kristine took Bertha (my name for the Suburban) out for a spin with the ladies. Later that evening, the ladies commented that she drove the vehicle better than I did. That was not a wise statement, considering I was driving Bertha, and all eight seats were occupied. Well, after shifting on the fly to four-wheel drive, I drove straight up the nearest sand dune, leaving no doubt, amid the screams, about who drove Bertha the best!

When we were not driving on the beach, we would rent ATVs and take turns riding them across the beach and adjacent sand dunes. I am not sure why I rode the way I rode. Maybe it was in search of a thrill, maybe it was in search of being alive, but I was reckless, and I went as fast as I could, spun donuts at the drop of a hat, and searched for jumps in my quest for the biggest air. Everyone worried for my safety. One day in particular, my nephew TK, Cheyanne, and I were out riding. On this occasion, I was especially reckless when I spied a large sand dune and headed toward it at maximum speed. When I flew off the sand dune, becoming airborne, I knew I was in trouble and while in the air, separated myself from the ATV to avoid landing on it awkwardly and possibly seriously hurting myself.

Beyond that, being on the beach and in the pool, shopping in the local markets, and of course, eating great food were the norms. Quinton wasn't even a year old on his first trip with us to Rocky Point, and it became his favorite place. Our trips to Rocky Point took on a special significance after Ed, my father-in-law, transitioned on June

8, 2003. Ed had been a family patriarch since at a young age when he saw his immediate family come apart through divorce. Ed and Nellie often vacationed in Rocky Point before Kristine and I married, and not long after we were married, we would often join them. If I was tied up working or taking a real-estate license class, Kristine and Cheyanne would go without me. I find it difficult now to come to terms with those missed trips. I was so absorbed in being what I thought society expected of me, so focused on having more stuff or just trying to make myself feel good about myself that I would forgo those trips.

After Ed's transition, Kristine and I discussed returning to Rocky Point, and Nellie agreed. We were both a little nervous when we approached Nellie; we really didn't know if she would ever want to go back to the place that Ed and she had loved, but she was eager to return. The annual trip to celebrate Ed's life became a trip we looked forward to every year. All of us—Quinton, Cheyanne, Kristine, Nellie, me, and sometimes our nephews—went on the annual trips to rocky Point aka Puerto Penasco. We looked forward to these vacations all year long. Often, we would talk about the next year's trip immediately after completing a vacation. This trip meant so much to us for a couple of reasons; first, it gave us a chance to spend time together, and second, it gave us a much needed break.

I, for one, lived for these vacations. Invariably, they were the only breaks I gave myself. During the year, I was singularly focused on my job and, more often than not, was a slave to our Conifer home on the weekends. I was typically the first one into the office and routinely gone from home for twelve to fourteen hours a day including commute during the week. On the weekend, I worked in the yard, raking, chopping wood, collecting and hauling slash, washing windows. . . and the list goes on. I rarely allowed myself time to enjoy living in scenic Colorado or even enjoy the family that I am blessed to be a part of.

Living in Conifer is like being in heaven to me. Our home is nestled in the pines at about 8,900 feet above sea level. Picturesque and beautiful both are adjectives that apply equally well. It was here that I had always wanted to raise my family after meeting, courting, and marrying Kristine in Phoenix, Arizona. Summers are glorious in Conifer, which is usually fifteen degrees cooler than Denver. Autumns can be equally as amazing as the aspens change, and Indian summer can last as long as a month or more during September and October; at this altitude, the warm period after the first freeze does sometimes last longer than you might expect. Winters are beautiful as well; there is nothing like the color of the blue sky after a snow storm. I often go outside after the snow ends and enjoy the view of the snow-laden pines with the crystal clear blue sky as a backdrop. Unfortunately, it wasn't until after Quinton transitioned and I internalized Quinton's messages that I began to appreciate our home and surroundings.

Before the accident opened my eyes, I was living a lie; I was deceived. Due to the way I was raised, I looked to my job and to how others thought of me for my self-worth. I gave the best of what I had to offer the world to my job and had nothing left for my family in the evenings and on the weekends. My priorities were completely reversed. Not anymore. The lie, the deception, the illusion has been shattered finally and forever. Now I am essentially unemployable on many levels. I am pleased to share the knowledge I have about efficient commercial office building operations. I give that knowledge freely, and I often save whatever owner I am working for tens of thousands of dollars, all the while laughing when I say out loud or think to myself, "You expect me to be concerned, be nervous, or work extra hours because of this?" Usually in the context of reporting, lease administration, bookkeeping, and accounting requirements, I often find some operations so fixated on the administrative side of managing properties that they completely neglect the operational side, which is where asset value is more often generated.

But at that time before Quinton left us, the once-a-year vacation washed the deception of who I thought I was or was supposed to be away, at least for a week or so. We were a family again, or to be more honest about it, I was part of the family again. We were so excited as the vacation approached. I would work at a feverish pace to clear my desk (to the extent that it could ever be empty) so I could go on vacation and not think about work. As the trip neared, Kristine typically packed more than we needed. I told her that all I needed was a bathing suit, a set of workout clothes, and a pair of shorts. The day would come, and I would get off work a little early to be home by 4:00 p.m., and we would leave.

Driving to Phoenix, Arizona, from Conifer, Colorado, in the summer is always a joy, because the days are long; leaving at 4:00 p.m., gave us approximately five hours of daylight. We almost always took Highway 285 to Del Norte and then Highway 160 until we were just outside of Flagstaff, Arizona. Six hours into the trip was our halfway point, and it left us in Cortez, Colorado. Depending on how I felt, we would either spend the night in Cortez or keep driving. I have always loved driving in the night because of the reduced traffic, but on the downside, the elk and deer came out at night in Colorado. We had to be ever vigilant to avoid them when they crossed the highway in the Colorado portion of our trip.

We would arrive at Ed and Nellie's home in the early morning on a Saturday or a Friday, rest for a day, and then leave for a three-and-a-half-to four-hour drive to Rocky Point. Over the years, our stay in Rocky Point usually began on Sunday, which was of great benefit, because we were going opposite the traffic flow. For the residents of Tucson and Phoenix, Rocky Point was a weekend getaway. Residents of those Arizona cities and surrounding towns took long weekends by leaving on Thursday night or Friday morning and returning to Arizona on Sunday. We would arrive in Rocky Point when the Arizonans were leaving, and we would be leaving when they were arriving.

The short trip between Phoenix and Rocky Point was not without its perils with so many of us Americans in a hurry and driving with reckless abandon on the way to a piece of heaven. That piece of heaven could be down on the beach or actually transitioning to pure energy as the result of a traffic accident on the way there. The latter is just what happened one year; somebody was making a dangerous pass, which resulted in a head-on collision. The accident happened about fifteen miles farther up the road than where we were, and we ended up parked in the desert for three hours while paramedics worked the sad scene. Fortunately, we were impacted by accidents only once, but I know that, at any time, it could have been me and my family.

When we arrived every year, Rocky Point was glorious. The tension mostly washed away from me during the drive, and any remaining tension vanished upon arrival. The yoke and the burden lifted and were replaced with a sense of peace, a sense of lightness. We would unload the Suburban and settle in by heading to the beach or pool.

Quinton and Cheyanne both loved the pool—any pool for that matter. In 1994, we bought a larger home to accommodate the large family we thought we would have and had a pool installed. Cheyanne grew up in that pool and started swimming at eighteen months. Quinton, on the other hand, only had access to a pool during vacations or on an occasional trip to the recreation center, but he loved the pool even more than Cheyanne. Year after year, Quinton spent every day of our vacations in the pool for as long as he could. He didn't care for the ocean that much. These vacations were perfect. We were in and out of the pool and in and out of the ocean; we rode rented Jet Skis, rode horses, and sat in the sun trying to reclaim our color.

Working out is one of the most enjoyable activities in my life, so when away from the grind of providing for my family and defining myself by my job, I always try to work out. This is something that I do for me, because I enjoy it. As Quinton became older, he insisted on working out with me while on vacation. The last two times we went to Rocky Point (June of 2007 and June of 2008), Quinton came to the resort gym with me. It is a struggle to explain just how much I enjoyed these sessions, but in an attempt to, let me just say that these sessions were the most important part of the vacation to me. I enjoy working out, and Quinton enjoyed working out with me. To be even more honest, Quinton enjoyed being with me and I with him—period. We would work out together with me checking his form and praising his efforts. He would beam with love; that is the way life should always be. When we decided to vacation on Lake Powell in 2009, the realization that Quinton and I would not be working out together during the vacation really bothered me. Maybe on some level, I understood our time spent working out together were all together through.

When we weren't running around enjoying every moment, we would just sit around and enjoy each other's company. Often I would read, but there were a lot of card games, some music, and a state of bliss. The picture of Quinton in a yoga pose says it all.

Ernie Jackson

Q—yoga pose

Sometimes these vacations flew by in a blink of an eye, and other times they seemed to last forever, but they were always perfect, except for our last Rocky Point vacation with Quinton. In 2008, Cheyanne, Kristine, and I were sick. We had some kind of upper respiratory crud that took us two months to shake. Nellie and Quinton were healthy. Cheyanne and Kristine were getting over it, but I was feeling miserable. It was still nice to get away, but I was a little bit angry. There I was on the vacation I had looked forward to all year, and I was sick. I was able to get some sun and read, but otherwise I tried not to get anybody else sick and slept during the second half of the week. During the first half of the week, I did work out once and rode Jet Skis as I attempted to do what I was accustomed to doing.

One of our favorite activities while on vacation was riding rented quads. We did this every time in Rocky Point, beginning before Ed was called home. We usually rented two quads and took turns. By the time Cheyanne had turned seven, we let her ride by herself. On her first time alone, she rode through clumps of tall grass and didn't realize that they were hills too. She hit one head on and was almost thrown over the handlebars. She cut her chin and was scared that we wouldn't let her ride again, but we did, and she never rode through the tall grass again. I was always reckless on the quad; I went as fast as I could, took jumps, and spun donuts until I was dizzy. On the trips when TK came with us, he followed my lead as we looked for the edge of the envelope. The older I became, the more I realized that I was an accident waiting to happen. Sure enough, the less reckless I was, the more close calls I had.

While Quinton enjoyed speed in my Camaro at the age three, he did not like going fast at all as he became older, and the same was true on a quad or Jet Ski. The 2009 vacation was going to give Quinton his first attempt to ride a Jet Ski or quad by himself. He shared with Cheyanne that he had been imagining steering the Jet Ski in the ocean.

Chapter Four

VACATION 2009

Preparation

Our 2009 vacation was different from the start, beginning with the vacation planning. Come the spring of 2009, we were undecided where we would go. The concern was the swine flu and the drug gang activity in Mexico. The extended family was pretty divided on whether or not vacationing in Rocky Point would be safe. Even the family of Cheyanne's friend Layla Voldrich, whom Cheyanne had asked to come along with us, was against Rocky Point. I took a harder line for a couple of reasons; I needed my vacation for reasons already discussed, and dying from swine flu or being shot by thugs didn't worry me.

At the height of my frustration, I said, "Okay. I will go to Rocky Point by myself."

Kristine looked at me incredulously and asked, "Really, you would go without us?" and then she immediately said, "Not likely."

My threat wasn't just bravado, although it sounds like it. I was at a point in my life when I was beginning to check out. I always thought I had some special abilities related to how, at times, I can "touch" a person with my energy. I thought I was destined to do more than what I was doing, to have a greater impact on those around me.. I had reached the point that I was at a loss as to how to do so, and I think I was starting to give up. This was the depth of my despair.

Ernie Jackson

The past year had been tough for me in commercial real-estate management, and I could not figure out what I was supposed to be doing with my life. I kind of figured that my work was done, and I was beginning to live through my son. All of this put me in the mind-set that, if I died while on vacation, so be it. Yeah, I know; that's selfish and warped, but that is where I was. I went so far as to plainly state that I was going to Rocky Point alone.

Damn it, I had earned my vacation, I needed my vacation, and I am going to take it . . . with my family or without my family, I thought to myself. I would have too, but cooler heads prevailed, and it is important to note that we changed our plans in an effort to avoid death. This was the first of many ah-ha moments.

In a prior year, one of Cheyanne's friends had asked if our family would accompany her family on its yearly vacation to Lake Powell, which was unrealistic at the time, given our annual trip to Rocky Point. In the spring of 2009 while Cheyanne was in Mrs. McNeil's English class, the class discussed how dangerous Mexico had become. Knowing that I was adamant about going there, Cheyanne called Kristine in a moment of frustration and said, "Why don't we go to Lake Powell instead of Rocky Point?" Kristine and Cheyanne continued this conversation when she came home from school and related the wonderful experiences her friend had shared. The decision to go to Lake Powell began to solidify as they discussed renting a houseboat.

Well, I had been to Lake Powell as a younger man, and I knew how beautiful the area was. I reluctantly agreed but with reservations. The prospect of doing something different didn't sit well with me. I expected that renting a houseboat would be work for me. Truthfully, I didn't want to learn anything new just so I could go on vacation; I wanted to be on autopilot. Going to Lake Powell meant training and being responsible to keep the family safe in unfamiliar conditions to the extent that was the Lord's will. Sure enough, the vacation turned out to be work.

We had been advised how wonderful being in a houseboat on Lake Powell was, but we suggested that, for the best time, we should have a

Jet Ski or two. Well, we don't own any, which meant that we would have to rent or borrow some. I wasn't keen about the expense of renting Jet Skis for a week, nor was I thrilled with the idea of towing any behind us. A few weeks prior to the trip, Kristine and Cheyanne went to the Marshdale Elementary School rummage sale, and an acquaintance offered the use of his Jet Skis. What a coincidence. But they declined, because they really didn't know him well, and being responsible for his Jet Skis made them nervous. Not long afterward, the Rodriguez family had a birthday party for their daughter, Morgan. Kristine and Cheyanne had gone out with them several times on their Jet Skis, so they decided to ask the Rodriguezes if we could borrow their Jet Skis. They graciously agreed.

While the vacation was coming together nicely, there was an undercurrent that wasn't the usual vacation excitement. Maybe it was the fact that all of us were out of our comfort zone because we were doing something different. I am not sure what it was, but most of us felt it. Being the most oblivious one of us all, I am often not aware of what is going on around me, but even I was uneasy. I felt change coming so strongly, I even cleaned out my office. That was a pretty bold move; I didn't plan on quitting and had nothing planned if I lost my job, but I still quietly removed almost all of my personal possessions a little at a time after the staff went home each day. I found this very odd, especially afterward. I do think this was the second ah-ha moment.

In addition to the above mentioned undercurrent, I went on the vacation looking for a message. This was a very conscious thought, I was looking for something and I even went so far as to put it out there in the universe. I was desperate for a message. I had been journaling off and on over the years by typing Word documents, but I had recently started a handwritten journal in that notebook. I hoped that something would come to me while out on Lake Powell in land sacred to the American Indians. I hoped for a message indicating what I should be doing with my life.

Cheyanne and Nellie both were uneasy, and Nellie almost didn't go. Both of them are more in tune with the universe, and something made them nervous. But we went anyway, and as I mentioned previously, Cheyanne brought her best friend, Layla Voldrich. None of us anticipated what would happen, but how could we have?

The day before we left, I took our 2007 Suburban over to the Rodriguezes' home to pick up the trailer with two Jet Skis. Our friends had spent time and money to make sure the Jet Skis were operational and safe, and we had even met them on Chatfield Lake the prior week to test-drive the skis, because we were forever trying to be safe. We attached the trailer, and they told me not to go over sixty miles per hour. They also told me not to worry if something happened on the lake. I was plainly told that, if the Jet Skis began to fill with water, I should just let them sink, because they were insured. I bristled at the thought of that! They were honoring us and trusting me with their recreational equipment, and I would be damned if I let anything happen to the skis. I told them so, and I meant it. I would keep their equipment safe, come hell or high water. We left the following evening at 7:10 p.m.

The Drive to Lake Powell

I got off work at 4:00 p.m. on Wednesday June 3 and picked up straps and jumper cables for the Jet Skis and red tape for a missing trailer light cover. I made it home around five thirty and then started packing our food and gear. All of us loaded the back of the Suburban, and whatever could not fit, we put on the front of the trailer. After all was secure, we walked around and around the rig to make sure that we weren't forgetting anything and that everything appeared safe. We climbed into the vehicle, and away we went, leaving Conifer for the last time as a family of four.

The drive was slow—painfully slow in my mind. We took the usual route that we took when traveling to Phoenix, leaving Conifer on Highway 285 to Del Norte and then taking Highway 160 through Four Corners. I have made this drive dozens of times, starting in May of 1986. It had always been the same—approximately, three hours from Conifer to Del Norte and another three hours from Del Norte to Cortez. This drive, however, seemed to take forever. About an hour past Del Norte while passing Devil's Creek just north of the Southern Ute Indian Reservation at three thirty in the morning, Cheyanne and Layla became uneasy. They both looked at the sign identifying the creek and then at each other. Cheyanne's anxiety level foreshadowed future events.

Not long afterward, we experienced our first flat tire on the trailer. It was pitch black, and there was no shoulder. After climbing out of the vehicle, assessing the situation, and coming up with a flashlight, I proceeded with changing the tire while on Highway 160. Along came an eighteen wheeler, and I thought, *Well, maybe it is my time to die.* I actually had that thought. I wasn't scared and didn't move quickly out of the way but kept on working.

Inside the Suburban, Cheyanne experienced similar feelings. In those crucial moments on the highway, she had thoughts of the semi taking out the driver side of the vehicle, leaving Kristine, Nellie, Layla, and myself unharmed, but taking Quinton and herself. The truck driver saw us and never came close. Looking back now, Cheyanne believes this was her way of saying, "I'm not ready to say good-bye. Envisioning us going together was more comforting."

At 4:00 a.m. we were moving again and thinking the worst was behind us. After we stopped in Bayfield for thirty minutes of sleep, we came through Cortez at 6:00 a.m. The town was pretty quiet, and most of the stores were closed. While we were cruising along thirty-one miles outside of Cortez and just a few miles from the Four Corners Monument, with visions of being on the water in a couple of hours, Kristine asked, "Do you feel that? Do you feel that vibration?"

"Yes," I said with a dejected voice. "I think we have another flat tire."

We did have a second flat tire and no spare. While we were in a state of disbelief, we held it together. We detached the trailer, removed another flat tire from the passenger side of the trailer, and headed back to Cortez with two flats after calling AAA, who informed us that a store that could help us would not be open until 8:00 a.m. We purchased two tires, and after they were installed on the rims, we headed back to the trailer.

Ernie and Quinton—changing tire on trailer.

Amazingly, we were in good spirits. Jokingly, I said, "Wouldn't it be great if the trailer was stolen?" Even then, so early in our trip, I was anxious to be done with it. We were almost disappointed when we pulled up to where we had left the trailer and it was still there. Quinton helped me put a tire on the trailer and affix the spare. Away we went through Kayenta; we finally arrived in Page, Arizona, by noon. What a long trip. We were tired but happy to finally be there. We all looked forward to anchoring the houseboat and relaxing.

Lake Powell Day One (Thursday, June 4)

We pulled up to the Wahweap marina, and their staff there was great. They helped us unload our stuff from the Suburban and onto our rented houseboat. They gave us a tutorial on what to do and what not to do. I tried to get anybody else in our group to partake in this tutorial, but everyone left it to me, just as I had feared they would. Much to my surprise, I retained the majority of what I was told; however, nobody else knew anything about how to operate the boat.

After the completion of the instructions, we were just about ready to cast off, but first we had to unload the Jet Skis. We left Nellie in the houseboat, which was still moored at the marina, and all of us went to the ramp. Inserting the plugs on the rear of the Jet Skis was relatively painless. Then we backed the trailer into the water. Kristine and Quinton drove the Suburban back to the marina. I drove one Jet Ski, and Cheyanne and Layla drove the other back to the marina. We rode the Jet Skis to the filling station at the marina to top them off with fuel. After fueling, we pulled into the marina.

"Does the Jet Ski seem low in the water?" I asked the girls. They both agreed. After opening the seat, I realized that it was taking on water. I never did know why, but we quickly decided not to take it with us. As I reflect back, I was exasperated, but I did not have a demonstrative outburst like I had been prone to for most of my adult life. I was on vacation and my attitude was that I wasn't going to let anything derail my time away from the grind. Kris drove the vehicle and trailer back to the ramp while I rode the Jet Ski back. We loaded it up, pulled the plugs out to drain the water, and then parked the rig at the Marina. Finally, we were ready to go.

With a sense of relief and great anticipation of an amazing week on the water, we backed the houseboat out of the marina, tied off the remaining Jet Ski, and headed directly across the lake to the closest beach we could find. We were tired and looking forward to anchoring and then relaxing for the rest of the afternoon.

Because it was the first time we had anchored the houseboat, we were all surprised that it went fairly smoothly. We had plenty of room to maneuver and came to the shore without incident. Slowly We pulled straight in to shore after scouting for an area deep enough to keep the twin motors in the rear of the boat above the lake bottom. After finding the right spot on the beach, we pulled in until the front pontoons gently touched bottom and then gunned it as instructed during the training session.

After making sure we were perpendicular with the beach, I set the motors at about two thousand rotations per minute, climbed out, set the anchors, let out a sigh, and started to unwind. The late afternoon sun was still high in the sky, and the weather was warm; the superficial stress from the drive melted out of our bodies. We hadn't bought fishing gear yet, so we lowered the gang plate, stepped off the boat, and walked around the beach for a while.

The girls had more energy and asked, "Can we take the Jet Ski for a spin?"

"Sure," I said.

They untethered it and rode it together in our immediate vicinity. The rest of us just lounged around, absorbed in the beautiful surroundings. That night, as the water rose, we felt the boat rock in the waves. The rocking comforted and further relaxed all of us. All of us slept like babies, gently rocking on the water.

Lake Powell Day Two (Friday, June 5)

The next day, we woke to a beautiful, sunny day. It was at this point that we really let the beauty of the area sink in. Some of us sat inside the houseboat, surveying the landscape away from the flies, and some of us sat outside the enclosure. All of us adults did so while holding cups of hot coffee. After a while, the ladies started breakfast.

Cheyanne, Layla, and Quinton were anxious to get in the water and did so after breakfast. The kids took turns riding around on the Jet Ski for a while, which was great fun. Even I hopped on for a quick spin. All of us rode in the immediate vicinity of the houseboat. The lake was so large that none of us wanted to get too far away for fear of getting lost. There was a sense of something unknown and larger than ourselves just around the corner as we enjoyed the morning into early afternoon.

Eventually, we secured our gear and prepared to relocate. There was only one problem: we were stuck, and I mean really stuck! We tried for at least thirty minutes to dislodge ourselves from the beach, and we ended up almost parallel with the beach and still stuck. We began wondering if we would need to call for help, but we weren't ready to give up yet. I asked Kristine to man the helm, and I got on the Jet Ski, which I was able to use to get us straightened out. I slowly drove the Jet Ski up to and against the rear of the boat on the side closest to the shore and gunned the motor. I was able to straighten out the boat, but we were still stuck. After shoveling around the front of the pontoons, it seemed that we were close to freeing ourselves.

So I told Kristine, "Put the engines into reverse while we push."

Cheyanne, Layla, and I pushed against the front of the boat for all we were worth while standing in the water up against the beach. Cheyanne poked fun at this idea.

"Do you really think we are going to push the boat?"

But we did! The boat was free, but now it was going backward at an alarming speed.

Kristine panicked, and I screamed at the top of my lungs, "Take the engines out of reverse." Eventually, she succeeded and had the twin motors going forward. Remember that nobody else had paid attention during the tutorial session.

Well, Kristine was going toward the beach at an alarming speed, and I was still screaming, but this time to take the engines out of forward movement. I could see being stuck again as well as lucky if we didn't tear the houseboat up. She reversed the motors at the last second before hitting the beach. With the motors going full tilt in reverse once again, I was able to grab a hold of the boat before it raced away again, and I dragged my body onto the boat to man the helm and bring order to the scene. What an adventure! It didn't take us long to find the comedy in it all. If someone had been video recording the scene, we surely would have won an award on *America's Funniest Home Videos*.

After securing the Jet Ski, we headed to the larger part of the lake, attempting to read the map and understand the buoys. Because we could do neither, we missed the cutoff and headed toward Glenn Canyon Dam. We took our time noticing the rock formations as we figured out where we were and where we were headed. The colors were amazing—different shades of beige with orange and red tints. The land was contoured and contained gullies that would no doubt fill with water when it rained . . . water that would cascade into Lake Powell. They were easy to spot, because the color of the rock in those locations was faded from erosion caused by the runoff. I pointed the gullies out and explained to Quinton and Kristine what they were seeing.

The girls either napped or were on the upper deck looking for boys in other boats. We must have cruised along for three or four hours at about 3,500 rotations per minute, which we were directed not to exceed. This RPM kept us between twenty and twenty-Five miles per hour; I for one wished were going faster! As we cruised, the breeze became a wind, and the waves were becoming larger. We began looking for a place to settle in for the night. We found a small cove with multiple landing sites; most of them made me nervous because they were too shallow. After we finally settled on one, we ended up hitting the beach so hard that dinner almost flew off the stove. I thought I had it figured out. Well, maybe not. Once again, I set the motors to keep the boat secure against the beach while we set the anchors.

This time, the Cheyanne and Layla asked, "Do you want us to help with the anchor holes?"

I was grateful for the offer. I started digging one while they started another. As I watched them, I provided guidance.

"Dig the hole a little deeper and wider," I said, and when the hole was just right, I told them, "Okay now, drop the anchor into the hole like I did mine." They came over to my hole to see what I meant. I covered my anchor with dirt and went over to help them cover theirs. We were done.

Not long after we finished, another, larger houseboat came into the cove to settle into a spot that we had avoided because it seemed just a bit too tight. I had thought my landing was rough, but I didn't feel so bad about it after watching and listening to them. We tried not to stare, point, and laugh out loud as they put on a show. They had untethered the boat they were pulling, and a couple of them were barking directions to the driver of the houseboat from the smaller boat. It really was comical as they barked, "You are going too fast. You need to straighten out. Watch out. You are going to crash into the shore," for what seemed like fifteen minutes. Eventually, they settled in, and the evening became calm. We spent two nights in this location—the night of Friday, June 5 and all of Saturday, June 6.

During the day on Friday and before the landing described above,, I picked up two fishing rods and assorted gear. What a fiasco that was. After getting the houseboat out of the sand, I left the houseboat—note to all people vacationing on Lake Powell, the captain is not supposed to leave the craft—I told them to stay put in the lake while I took the Jet Ski in to the marina and bought the gear.

At this point, it began to sound a little like a Bill Cosby skit when I say that, apparently, I should have told them to leave the motors running. I was eventually reunited with them after they were brought to shore by patrol. I asked for help locating them after riding back and forth across the lake near where I had left them. The day had clouded over, and I was freezing as the breeze blew water in my face. Finally, I found a shore patrol and asked for their assistance in finding my family and heard, "Oh, you must be the captain who left his boat." Yup, that was me.

After I left the boat, they had turned the motors off and thought they would float in place, and then they didn't know how to start them. *And this is a vacation*? I wondered. They were petrified as they floated closer and closer to a large rock outcropping.

"What would grandpa do in a situation like this?" Quinton asked Nellie.

Fortunately, Cheyanne and Layla got on the radio, and help arrived before they crashed into the rocks.

Lake Powell Day Three (Saturday, June 6)

I had planned on fishing while on vacation. I proudly tell everyone that I go out to practice my casting. The sun rose on a cloudless day. When I was the first one up at approximately 6:00 a.m., I quietly went outside, baited my hook, and started casting with the typical results. Squinting into the sun, I could make out the bobber in the water; it had no activity at all. I reeled in the rig a couple of times to check the bait and to cast to different locations around the boat. Eventually, I picked up a book that I brought and started reading while the bobber floated in the water. I occasionally peeked over the top of the book to see if the bobber was where it should be.

One time when I looked up, the bobber was gone! *What is this?* I pondered. Much to my surprise, a fish had hooked itself, and all I had to do was reel it in. It was an eleven-inch smallmouth bass! Wow. I had never caught a bass before, and I was excited. By then, everyone was waking up, and they came to see the catch. Later that day, I cleaned and filleted it before cooking it in foil with onions, tomato, and seasoning. Kristine and I laughed as we each had a mouthful. It was good but not enough for a meal.

No more fish were caught at that location, but we had a good time. There was a lot of Jet Skiing, lounging in the sun, and swimming. The day seemed to last forever as we took turns on the Jet Ski. Everyone got a turn, except Nellie, who was perfectly content to stay safe and dry on the houseboat. Cheyanne and Layla spent a lot of time on the Jet Ski, but I was the first to find a small cove tucked into the hillside. After I showed Cheyanne, she showed Kristine and Layla. We took pictures, and I shot video of Kristine and Quinton on the Jet Ski.

Quinton was a little nervous on the Jet Ski with me. When we went out together, I could feel him tense up each time I goosed the throttle. He thought I went too fast; he had gotten to a point in his life when he did not like going fast. He wouldn't ride with me after that one time, but he enjoyed cruising with Kristine at a more reasonable speed. Even with Kristine at the helm Quinton would say, "Go slow, Mom. Be careful."

Eventually, we put the Jet Ski away because we were running low on fuel. At the time, we could not understand how we had gone through the fuel that quickly, but in retrospect, the Jet Ski had been ridden quite a bit, especially the day before as I had looked for my family.

We turned our attention to swimming. Quinton always wanted to be in the water, and he got visibly upset if nobody joined him. I fondly remember being the in water with him at that site. It was in the middle of the afternoon, and the weather had turned warm. Kristine and Nellie were napping, and the girls were sunning themselves. Quinton and I were in the back of the houseboat, when I turned to him.

"Do you want to swim to the other side?" I asked as I pointed across the cove. I really didn't have to ask, because I knew the answer would be yes. We put our vests on, jumped into the water, and began to swim across the cove. We took our time. It was a leisurely swim; as we stopped occasionally to look around. I watched for boats heading in our direction, but there weren't any.

As we neared the shoreline, my feet found the bottom before Quinton's did. Then we walked up the shore together and explored. Quinton would stop and say, "Look, Dad," as he pointed at interesting looking rocks. Quinton loved rocks of all shapes and sizes—the more colorful the better. While we walked around, he picked up some of the rocks that caught his eye, putting them into a pocket in his swim trunks. These are fond memories; I miss my son. We eventually walked back into the water and swam back to the boat.

Later in the afternoon, everyone's attention turned to the slide on the houseboat. Kristine had specifically reserved a houseboat with a slide, because we thought Quinton would love going down it, but he refused. Something was unsettling Quinton during the whole trip; he avoided anything that might result in a sudden impact with the water. Cheyanne and Layla made use of it.

While we were at this location, Quinton noticed a salamander walking on the anchor line toward the houseboat. All of us took turns watching it and trying to shake it off so it wouldn't end up on the boat with us.

Late that afternoon, Quinton and I played our last game of catch. I had purchased a small football while in the marina. I got it right thinking of how much Quinton would enjoy the ball as I purchased it. Kristine told me later that Quinton was delighted when he looked in the bag of fishing gear and saw the football and a small Frisbee. While we were on the beach, we threw that ball back and forth as the sun set. Quinton whipped that ball to me as I told him, "Q, you have an amazing spiral." Quinton always beamed when I praised him, and this time wasn't any different. He smiled back at me, and I smiled at him as we played our last game of catch. We could have played all night, but eventually, it became too dark to see, and we climbed back onto the boat for the evening. I still have that ball.

Lake Powell Day Four (Sunday, June 7)

On the morning of Sunday, June 7, we left the site without event (meaning we did not get stuck). We cruised slowly to the channel we had missed previously and back to Wahweap marina to refuel the Jet Ski. We parked the houseboat with other houseboats in the market marina, which was a feat I was quite proud of. The Kristine and Nellie resupplied as I took the Jet Ski for fuel. We met up afterward, and the girls rode the Jet Ski around the marina as I backed the houseboat out of the bay and into the open marina. We tied the Jet Ski to the back of the boat as we prepared to head to another location on the lake. With that done, we started searching for another spot, with the goal of being close to Wahweap for the rest of our vacation. I drove the houseboat, and I felt it dragging.

"Sweetheart, can you check on the Jet Ski?" I asked Kristine.

She left the front of the boat where we had sat together to check, and she came back out of breath, saying, "It is under water."

I stopped our forward motion and went back to check. Sure enough, it was almost completely submerged. We needed to get the swamped Jet Ski to shore.

"Can we drive it to shore?" the girls asked, but I saw that it was close to completely sinking, so I decided to drive it in myself—at that point, everybody knew how to drive the houseboat.

I donned my life jacket as visions danced in my mind of me in the middle of the lake without a life jacket if the Jet Ski sank. Somehow it started, and I headed back to shore while the rest of the group kept the houseboat motors running and maintained position. This decision had been made quickly, because I was determined not to lose our friends' Jet Ski.

I made it to shore and caught a ride back out to the houseboat with a group of people in their twenties. When I was back on the houseboat, we headed to the original marina we left from at the start of our vacation. We parked and went for the Suburban. Somehow, I got the Jet Ski started one last time and was able to get it onto the trailer, but it was full of water. After we loaded the Jet Ski onto the trailer and pulled the two plugs in the rear to drain the water, I could never start it again. We think water seized the motor.

Refusing to let this mishap and the others we had experienced dampen our spirits, we climbed back onto the houseboat and headed out once again. We cruised directly across from the marina and past our landing site from day one of our adventure. I was looking for a site a little farther west but still in sight of the marina when Layla spied a beautiful and private cove. It was secluded with green and calm water, a sandy beach on the east side of the cove, and a large rock outcropping on the west that cast a shadow across the cove. On that beautiful Sunday afternoon, we pulled to shore without turmoil and anchored the houseboat. Hey, maybe we had this figured out after all.

The sun continued to drop lower in the western sky, and soon we would be in shade. It was time for me to practice my casting again. I cast one fishing rod out for me and one out for Quinton. Initially, nothing happened, but then suddenly one of the bobbers was gone. No, it was not bobbing up and down; it was gone and showed no sign of returning. I grabbed the rod and started reeling in the line. Eventually, the bobber became visible while still under water. I kept reeling and, much to my amazement, reeled in an eighteen-inch catfish. The boat was abuzz as I put the fish in the cooler, placed a fresh worm on the hook, and cast out again. Five minutes later, another catfish was on the line; this one was fourteen inches. Wow. What a treat!

Kristine had started dinner earlier without expecting fresh fish. Another great dinner was ready when I cast out again. I was trying to rig the rod so that, if another fish hooked itself, the rod would not end up in the lake. As I did this, yet another fish was hooked on the line. I reeled it in and went in for dinner. We ate dinner quickly and then went back outside for more fishing.

The weather was beautiful, and the late afternoon sun bathed us in a soothing yellow light, but soon we would be completely in the shade caused by a small mountain on the west side of the cove.

"Who wants to catch a fish?" I asked.

"I do," Layla said, the first to respond.

After I baited her hook and cast it out for her, she was in business. She quickly caught a fish.

Cheyanne was next. She was a little nervous, and I think she was concerned about doing something wrong. I proved that she had reason to be nervous as I yelled, "Reel it in. Reel it in. You have a fish on the line." The fish escaped, and it seemed as if I ruined the experience for her, so I went into the houseboat while the girls rebaited the hook. Cheyanne caught her catfish while I wasn't watching, but Quinton was watching and commented to Kristine "Thanks to the Lord!" He knew that Cheyanne would be cranky if she didn't catch a fish too.

After I went back outside, I asked Quinton if he wanted to catch a fish, since he hadn't volunteered. Quinton's response was classic and, in hindsight, not a surprise.

"No, Dad," he said. "I have already done that."

Quinton was referring to the summer of 2008 when I had taken him to a trout farm at Shaffer's Crossing and Highway 285, which was not far from our home. On that summer day, he caught two trout, and I pronounced him the fisherman of the family. Quinton's response indicated that, since he had already had that experience in his life, he no longer needed to catch another fish. In retrospect, it was an interesting comment. The rest of the afternoon was spent swimming, eating, relaxing, and watching movies.

Lake Powell Day Five (Monday, June 8)

On Monday, June 8, the sun rose bright and even warmer than the previous days. I wore a hat to keep the sun and sweat out of my eyes as I scouted around the peninsula. There were a lot of ants and shells from when the lake had been higher. A large group of people had anchored on the other side, and I noticed that the water continued around a bend to another secluded cove. When we had noticed the entrance previously, it had looked like the cove ended, but we had been mistaken. I kept walking to find where the cove actually ended.

It was beautiful, and nobody was there. I found out that the cove was well-known because of what I called the sand slide. Between the rocks was a giant sand dune of the softest sand that rose about 500 feet from the bottom of the cove and was about thirty feet across. This sight was truly awe-inspiring and beautiful! On either side of the sand were sandstone rocks that kind of made the sand look like a waterfall that was no longer falling.

I went back to our houseboat and told the family about it, asking, "Who wants to see it?" Ever ready for a new adventure, Quinton was the first to accept. We took our time and walked over and then scouted around some more. He and I came back to the boat sweaty, and Kristine was ready next, so we went to take a look. All the while, we didn't see a soul. We decided that we would spend the rest of our vacation in that cove, but before we could do so, we had to resolve an issue with the boat's septic system. We realized there was an issue when the water from our showers was slow to drain and eventually didn't drain completely out of the shower basin. We headed back to the marina to have it pumped out.

We came back as quickly as we could so no one else could show up and claim the site that we wanted. When we got back to the cove entrance, it was narrow, so we took it slow. After we came around a right-hand turn and passed the group we had seen earlier, we entered the cove with our rented houseboat. At first, we thought of anchoring at the base of the sand slide, but we reconsidered, because it was a little tight. We chose the one other site, which was about fifty yards from the sand slide. This site had a rock wall on the west, just like the site we'd anchored at before. This rock wall was sheer, and part of it had a rock overhang that had already partially eroded in the past. We could see where the rocks had fallen, strewn across a portion of a perfect area for a campfire. We had been told that deaths had occurred when boats were anchored under loose rocks. We were eager to avoid that mistake, so we parked the houseboat away from the rock overhang.

It was afternoon, and Quinton was ready to get back in the water. The girls weren't quite so eager, and I was busy anchoring the boat. I distinctly remember Quinton being sad, but he grabbed his life jacket and jumped into the water alone. Quinton vacationed hard and often to the point of exhaustion.

The next two nights in that cove were a microcosm of the entire vacation. I watched the scenario play out as I anchored the boat. Seeing Quinton sad of course made me sad and a little annoyed that nobody had joined him in the water. I worked faster at setting the anchors so I could join him. After I finished, I was sweaty and out of breath, but I quickly grabbed my life jacket and jumped into the cove with my son, who was sad no more. The cool water was refreshing as we swam around and explored.

After a few minutes, I turned to Quinton and asked, "Do you want to climb up the sand hill?"

"Sure," he said and started over toward it.

On the way there we explored a smaller cove. Quinton and I both found the terrain fascinating—so much so that we climbed out of the water to explore on foot. After we satisfied our curiosity, we jumped back into the water, made it to the sand slide, walked out of the water, and began up the hill. Initially, the climb wasn't too difficult as we went up together, but about halfway up, the incline increased, and it seemed like we slid back two steps for each step forward. We took our time and ended up on all fours at the hill's steepest point.

As we climbed, we stopped as we noticed names and years carved into the sandstone. The oldest were from the early eighties. We had been warned against doing the same when we had arrived at Lake Powell, but clearly many before us either hadn't received the same warning or hadn't cared about defacing the rock.

When we finally made it to top, we were ecstatic. I said something to the effect of, "Quinton, I am so proud of you. Look at what you have accomplished. After doing this, you can do anything." That was a moment I will never forget. I was often pleased with my son, whether while playing catch or basketball or just being together. This was our last conquest together while Quinton was with us in body. He replied, "I know, Dad." We enjoyed our time at the top of the hill looking around and down upon the rest of the family. They seemed so small as they looked up at us. Kristine took several pictures, and one of them ended up on a picture board and slideshow at the celebration of Quinton's life.

Q and EJ beginning their climb

Q and EJ nearing the top

After a while, it was time to come down. I suggested to Quinton that we lean back as we bounded down, and we started our descent laughing and smiling the whole way down. We were warm once more by the time we arrived at the cove, so we eagerly waded into the water and were soon back on the houseboat.

Before dinner, the girls were ready for the hill, or they thought they were. There wasn't a question of whether or not Quinton would go with them—the hill was his! Cheyanne, Layla, and Quinton meandered over to the sand. Quinton stayed in the water while the girls tried to get to the sand without getting wet. The rest of us were in the houseboat as I recorded with our video recorder. This was yet another example that Quinton walked among us as an angel; he was always concerned about the welfare of others. The girls ended up in a precarious position on the rock above the cove. They could not go up any farther. The seconds became minutes, and the girls started to panic.

"Slide straight down on your butt," we yelled over to Layla.

"But I will fall," she said.

"Into the water," we added.

Quinton waited in the water. The water was cold, and he was becoming cold, but he would not return to the boat or go to shore. He stayed there, shivering, but he would not leave them. As Cheyanne became aware that her brother was cold, she no longer wanted to assist her friend in getting down from the rocks.

Exasperated, she said to Layla, "Just sit on your back side and slide down. Suck it up. Q has been waiting. My brother is cold."

Eventually, the girls came down off the rocks and jumped into the freezing water that they had hoped to avoid and the same water that Quinton had been in for fifteen minutes. They made it to shore and started up the hill. As they rose in elevation, they came out of the shade caused by the rocks to the west of the hill. The girls laughed and warmed up in the sun as they made it up the hill. Quinton also laughed and warmed up.

He waited for the girls when they became tired and lay in the soft sand. Quinton made it to the top again and waited again for the girls. We were actually surprised that they toughed it out and made it to the top.

Quinton led the way down, just like I had showed him, without falling. Layla, on the other hand, wiped out in a spectacular way. We thought she was trying to fall to be silly, but she knocked the wind out of herself and took a few minutes to recover.

Back into the boat they came for dinner and movies. It was Monday, June 8, which was the anniversary of my father-in-law's transition, and we celebrated Ed Cano's transition by having Quinton's favorite meal, chicken fettuccini, and his favorite beverage, root beer. For dessert, Kristine made brownies, and Quinton added white and blue shark candies on top.

That night, we watched one of Quinton's favorite movies, *Madagascar*. Everyone except Cheyanne watched it; she had gone to the upper deck of the boat by herself. We generally relaxed and had a nice time. Everything seemed right in our world. Like every evening, we spent it sitting around the dinner table, talking, laughing, and playing cards, until it was movie time.

At that point, everyone found a place to sit or lay down. On this evening, Layla was on the dining room table now converted to a bed by herself. I noticed that Quinton was perched precariously on a couch arm, so I said, "Quinton, go and sit by Layla. There is plenty of room next to her." He wasn't having any of it. He looked at me shyly and shook his head from side to side. Eventually, I picked him up and set him by her, but he was there for not even a second before he went back to his perch.

Quinton left us with his innocence intact. He had no desire to be near a pretty girl, even if they had spent what seemed like hours together in the lake. Layla was another person who had a bond with Quinton, but that didn't mean he would sit next to her during movie time.

Afterward, Cheyanne shared, "I will always regret my stubborn will for not spending this night with my family."

Later that night, after we went to bed, the wind came up. I was up several times to check the mooring lines and our position against the shore. Fortunately, we never came loose. During the houseboat tutorial, I had made a joke about not wanting to wake up floating loose on the lake; the gentleman giving the tutorial had not laughed. In hindsight, I understand why he didn't think my joke was funny.

Lake Powell Day Six (Tuesday, June 9)

Even I slept in the next morning. My dreams have always been fuzzy at best, and typically, I could not even remember my dreams. Any dreams that I might have had were during my REM sleep, and usually, I would estimate, no later than four thirty in the morning, which makes sense, given that my alarm usually went off at 5:00 a.m. On Tuesday, June 9, it was significantly different in time of day and clarity of my dreams. This was the third ah-ha moment. I had a vision of my son passing away.

At 7:00 a.m., I had a crystal clear dream/vision. In my vision, Quinton and I were sitting together happily on the back of the houseboat within the very cove where we were then anchored. I was holding the right side rail with my right hand, and my left arm was around Quinton as we sat there swinging our feet in the water. Suddenly, a huge boat—not a houseboat, it looked like an ocean liner—came into our cove and swung an immediate 180-degree turn. This sudden turn sent a wave toward us that dwarfed our houseboat and completely swamped us. In my vision, Quinton and I went under water. My left arm, which was around Quinton, had been surgically repaired years before, and it was significantly weaker than my right. Quinton was patting me on my chest to let me know that he was struggling, but I couldn't do anything.

It was that helpless feeling that woke me up. Within an hour of waking, I told Quinton and Kristine about my dream. When I finished sharing the dream, Quinton said in a voice that sounded somehow older, "Dad, it wouldn't happen that way. I would just swim away." Something about how he said that was different.

I forgot about the dream and Quinton's statement until our private viewing of his perfect little body. When I remembered, I broke down yet again and cried as I realized that was exactly what he had done: he swam away into another realm.

The day had started out cooler than the others and slightly overcast. After I shared the dream, we stayed in the houseboat until we noticed a camera crew in the cove. At that point, we realized that we were in a well-known location on the lake. People had come and gone on a regular basis just to climb the sand hill. Most were friendly, and we waved when they passed. One group we bantered with asked to use the slide on the houseboat, and we invited them over. On that morning, though, it was just the camera crew from *The Weekend Explorer*.

Quinton and I went out and introduced ourselves.

"Hey, what are you doing?" we asked.

Jeff Lehman, the host of the show explained they were there to film a feature for one of their episodes, and were going to include this well-known site. Jeff was looking for volunteers to climb the hill with him while his cameraman recorded.

I trotted back to the houseboat and told the girls, "Hey, it's time to get up. This is your chance to be on television. This is your big opportunity."

They weren't having it. There was no time for them to put on makeup and do their hair, so only Quinton and I joined Jeff on the hill.

While I was trying to get Cheyanne and Layla up, Quinton and Jeff talked, and they connected in a way that we are still discovering as we put the finishing touches on this book.

Quinton's Messages

Q and EJ—Weekend Explorer at the sand slide

We climbed into the camera crew's boat and rode over to the base of the hill, because it was too cold to be in the water. We hopped out and started on our way. It quickly became evident that Jeff was in really good shape as we made our way up the hill. He led the way, and I did my best to keep up. I made up some ground at the steepest part of the hill, but I looked back and saw Quinton falling back, so I immediately stopped. Jeff stopped too. We finished the climb at a more leisurely pace and tried to collect ourselves at the top. Jeff didn't appear tired at all, but I was completely exhausted. I am sure I was red all over as I tried to catch my breath. Quinton was there with us as they recorded us waving at the camera from the top.

Then down we bounded as fast as we could. Jeff would not let me catch him. I was gaining quickly as we neared the bottom, but he sensed me and turned on the jets. I guess it would not have looked good for him to not be leading the way, given it was his show. What was I thinking?

We climbed back into the boat and then offloaded at our houseboat.

The girls were sufficiently made-up by then and were ready for some face time, so they took turns going down the slide while the weekend explorer camera was recording. All of us implored Quinton to do the same, but he refused. There was something about going down that slide that scared him.

At a couple of points during the vacation he almost went down the slide. The first time, he got on the slide but still wasn't ready to go down. I gave him a nudge, and he locked up, so I hauled him back up. Another time, he was intent to go but with his goggles on. After he put his goggles on, he walked determinedly to the slide. I cut him off, telling him, "Quinton, you cannot go down the slide with your goggles on, because when you hit the water, the goggles might cut your face or break your nose." He still wanted to go, but eventually Quinton dejectedly took off his goggles and again refused to go down the slide.

Not long after Jeff and his crew left, the day began to warm, and the sun came out. Back into the water for more swimming the kids went!

As the day proceeded, Kristine decided she also wanted to climb the hill. She was the only one who hadn't been up the hill, except for Nellie, and she knew we would give her a bad time if she did not give it a try. I am not sure what time it was, but it might have been around 3:00 p.m.

As the girls and Kristine talked about the climb, Quinton donned his life vest and was off. By the time Kristine, Cheyanne, and Layla made it to the shore, Quinton was a quarter of the way up the hill. He hadn't even taken off his life vest; he had just walked out of the water and marched up the hill. Quinton looked like a soldier marching with perfect form. I was recording with our video camera and marveled out loud at how amazing Quinton was.

By the time the girls were halfway up, Quinton had gotten to the top and was on his way down. He came down quickly, took his vest off, and started back up for his fifth and final time. Still marching, he passed the girls and crested the hill yet again. The girls were not even at the top yet. Quinton came back down, put back on his life vest, and walked back into the water. What a machine Quinton was. I was so proud of him.

As I continued to videotape, I called out to him. I didn't realize what I said until I finally watched the video in September 2009. Watching the video that first time left me with my mouth hanging open. I told him I was proud of him, and then I said, "Come on home." Why did I say that? I didn't remembered saying that, but Quinton's expression as I made that statement gave me a jolt. He looked confused, and he looked like he really didn't want to come home. That was one of the rare times he ignored me; he did not come back to the houseboat. He continued to tread water until Kristine, Cheyanne, and Layla came back down the hill. That was Quinton: he would not leave them. Yet again, he clearly demonstrated who he was in body.

They swam back to the houseboat together. Kristine was exhausted, but Quinton was still going strong. Later that afternoon, Quinton and the girls swam across the cove with their life jackets on. They just chilled on the other side as they talked and explored. Kristine took pictures, and there was one taken of Quinton standing on a barely submerged rock while the girls sat around it. Yes, indeed, it did appear that Quinton was standing on water.

That night was spent together as a family with more good food and movie watching, and it was the only night that Quinton slept in the same room as Kristine and me. During the whole vacation, the girls had slept on the upper deck, Quinton had slept with Nellie in a bedroom, and Kristine and I had slept on a hideaway bed in the family room. Quinton had insisted on sleeping with his grandmother, in part, because he was concerned that she could not get on the bed by herself. The bed was almost too high for Nellie, and often, Quinton would jump up first and then turn around and help Nellie up. All through the vacation, Quinton would go to sleep before Nellie, but he would tell her to wake him up when she came to bed so he could help her. Nellie didn't want to wake her grandson, so each night, she climbed up by herself. Every morning,

Quinton would wake up, look at Nellie, and ask, "Why didn't you wake me up?"

On the last night on the lake, Quinton inexplicably slept with us. We have said over and over that, on some level, Quinton knew his time was drawing near. Maybe that was why he slept with us one last time.

Chapter Five

THE END OF THE VACATION

On the morning of Wednesday, June 10, I was up early and ready to get my family home safely. For some reason, I put my contact lenses in not long after waking up. It made no sense, given that driving usually left me tired as did wearing my contacts, but I put them in with little a thought. I was recharged and ready to try yet again to balance myself between my family (which should be my only priority) and the job. I was looking forward to getting home, climbing Mount Bierstadt, and going to Bandimere Speedway with the family.

As usual, I was driven to leave as early as possible; I am not sure why. I just have a sense that, if we leave early, we can avoid issues or problems. As usual, the family was wondering why we were packing up at 9:00 a.m. We were heading back to the marina by 11:00 a.m.

"Hopefully, the road trip back home won't be as bad as the trip coming here," we said.

My eagerness for the drive was mixed with melancholy. Maybe it was a sadness that the vacation was over and that there would not be another vacation for a year. Everybody else felt it too as we rode, in relative silence, back to the marina for the last time. Quinton sat on the back of the houseboat, just sitting and looking at it all. He had done a lot of that on the vacation, much more so than usual. There are pictures of Quinton sitting and looking off into the expanse with a blank look on his face. We are certain that, on some level, Quinton knew what was coming. I thought we had it beat. At forty-four years old, I still had the illusion of control. I now know better.

Back in the Wahweap marina, we offloaded. Much to my surprise, the boat was in fine condition after our adventures, and we checked out without incident. We loaded our gear into the Suburban. It seemed that we still had a lot of stuff. It didn't all fit inside the Suburban, so the overflow (our two fishing rods, the Ab Roller, and a cooler) was once again tied down to the front of the trailer.

Before we left the parking lot, Quinton and I replaced the driver-side trailer tire, which had not failed on the drive in. We jacked up the trailer and loosened the lug bolts. As we pulled the tire off the trailer, I had another surprise: the condition of the tire was atrocious; the tread was delaminating from the tire. I was pleased with myself for changing it before it blew out.

With two brand-new tires on the trailer, we pulled out of Page, but before officially starting our drive home, we stopped by Wal-Mart and bought two brand-new tires and rims just in case. We were trying to be more than prepared, and I felt confident that we would make it home without incident. Cheyanne, on the other hand, had a nervous feeling, which manifested itself in the form of her not feeling well. She had butterflies in her stomach.

Heading east out of Page on Highway 98, we drove with traffic. We were passed often. It was unusual for me to be passed on a road trip, but we were trying to be safe. Still, we were having problems with the trailer. For some reason, the right tire was rubbing when we hit dips in the road. We stopped several times to adjust the Jet Skis' positions in an effort to shift the weight to the center of the trailer. Eventually, we added rolled up towels under the Jet Ski on the right in an effort to further shift the weight.

We made it to Highway 160, just south of Kayenta where 98 ended. I continued to drive while looking in two directions: watching the road in front of us and looking in the mirrors for any sign of smoke caused by tire rubbing. We drove through Kayenta, heading to Four Corners and the most improbable tragedy. We stopped twice more to adjust our load in an effort to prevent the right tire from rubbing against the trailer wheel well. Just past the Four Corners Monument, we had had enough. The rubbing was getting worse, and it was clear that we would be unable to make it all the way home.

We were barely into Colorado when I pulled into a wide-open dirt area adjacent to the highway. I thought we pulled over just past mile marker one, but the police report indicated it was mile marker three. On subsequent visits to this location, our initial thoughts are verified; it was mile marker one. The pull-out was huge—approximately one hundred yards by forty yards. We pulled into the area just past an orange road construction sign, and as soon as we left the pavement and drove onto the dirt, the trailer collapsed. The right axle snapped. Kristine knew immediately that something was wrong. We stopped thirty feet off of Highway 160 and got out of the vehicle.

Kristine and I went back to the trailer and knew the trailer would not be going any farther. I asked her to call the Rodriguez family before calling AAA. While she was on the phone with Joanne, I began to shift the load. I pulled the two new spares for the trailer out of the back of the Suburban and affixed them to the trailer with a bolt and nut for each. Kris finished her call and called AAA; soon, she was on the phone with Doug of Doug's Quality Towing in Cortez, which was approximately thirty-seven miles away. Quinton helped me some with the tires, but at some point, I lost track of him. Kristine remembers telling him to get back into the Suburban, and he did as he was told. Both Cheyanne and Nellie remember that he was inside the Suburban until just before God called.

Kristine does not remember anything after screaming. I am not sure what she said, and neither is she. I do remember the tone of that scream; it got my attention. Its tone and volume had never been heard before. Something was seriously wrong. I was on the passenger side of the trailer toward the rear with my back to the Cortez-bound traffic when the scream set me into immediate motion. As I was digesting the tone of the scream, I heard or sensed something else, but still didn't know what it was..

It all happened so fast, I didn't have time to be afraid. I didn't even have a moment to look at Kristine, who was also standing on the passenger side of the Suburban near the front. For some reason, I was desperate to turn and face whatever was coming. At forty-four years old, my old athleticism hadn't completely left me. I was instantly on my toes and turning, but as quickly as I reacted; it wasn't fast enough to face the nightmare headed straight for us. I only made a ninety-degree turn, which saved my life.

I will never forget that impact. As a former football player, I understand physical contact, but this was altogether different and had no comparison. I was fully in the moment when I took the hardest hit of my life on my left hip. It was like *kaboom* and then a moment of nothingness. At the time of impact, my eyes must have closed, and I don't remember landing. In a flash and eighteen feet away (right next to the rear passenger door of the Suburban), I opened my eyes to a scene that is still hard to believe. While I was in the air, the Pontiac Sunbird that had hit me continued under me, sideswiped the Suburban, and then drove over the top of Kristine as she tried to run to the safety that she thought the Suburban provided.

Surprise and disbelief were what I felt as my eyes opened. I was face down, on my stomach, and dust was swirling in the air. Everything was in slow motion. I saw Kristine's body and thought she was dead, because she lay crumpled and twisted. I saw Nellie running to Kristine, screaming. I immediately assumed the worst. Much later, I was told that she was screaming for me to help Kristine. As I took in this unbelievable scene before me, I saw the bumper of a car that I knew did not belong to our vehicle, and then I rolled over and looked behind me for some reason.

While I rolled over, I began doing an inventory of my own body to see if I was missing any body parts. Much to my surprise again, I was alive and everything was there. The rational part of my mind was preparing to apply a tourniquet to myself if necessary. While everything was there – our world had been turned upside down and inside out.

And then I saw Quinton, not at all understanding why he was where he was. He was between the trailer and the Suburban, lying motionless. It is odd how our minds work in a situation such as that. In a moment, I clearly recognized that Nellie was with Kristine and nobody was with my son. I dragged myself over to Quinton, not knowing what to expect. He had barely a scratch on his body. He had a gash over his left eyebrow, and his ankle was mangled, but he was breathing. The dirt in his open mouth, covering his braces, was the hardest to take, so I tried to ignore it. That bothered me more than anything. Why was there dirt in my son's mouth? Not only was it not right, it wasn't fair. I turned away from that aspect of an awful reality and fixated on his breathing in through his mouth and out through his nose. I noticed his eyes, but I didn't understand the significance of what I was seeing until later. Quinton's eyes were open, unblinking, and nonresponsive.

For the next twenty minutes, this sad, unimaginable, and improbable scene played out.

Cheyanne had the worst of it as she stepped out of the vehicle to find her entire immediate family lying in the dust and bleeding. Even though it is related here, I was not aware of her activity at the scene. My focus was Quinton. Our daughter, this young lady who had just turned sixteen on May 27 was in the process of having her world completely ripped apart. Cheyanne went to her mother, saw her eyes rolled back in her head, and foam coming from her mouth. Kristine looked dead to Cheyanne.

Cheyanne came over to Quinton and me and then began frantically calling 911 and babbling to the operator, trying to explain the unexplainable. She continued to go back and forth between her family members, feeling helpless. My daughter was desperately trying to get help. Some people stopped, getting out of their cars to either gawk or help. Many more kept on driving, not wanting any part of the painful scene. In any case, there were a lot of people at the scene of the accident.

Layla Voldrich was a rock. All of us knew there was something special about Layla—well, all of us except maybe Layla herself. Quinton got along so well with Layla, who asked the best questions. Layla took nothing for granted, and she was not at all afraid to ask a question that many would be too embarrassed to ask, which resulted in her having a lot of practical knowledge. While I knew how unique Layla was, I didn't know just how strong she was until that moment and in the coming days. She stayed there with me and Quinton. I was on one side of my son, and she was on the other as time seemed to drag on with Quinton still breathing but nonresponsive. We yelled encouragement to Quinton with no response, and we looked across Quinton's body into each other's eyes. I was bleeding from my forehead and from a cut between my eyes; blood was dripping down my face. Layla wiped away the blood as best as she could, and I thanked her for being there. She replied, "I only wish I could do more." When the paramedics started arriving, she left once to check on Kristine and comfort Cheyanne, but then she was right back there with Quinton and me.

Nellie stayed with Kristine and was unaware that Quinton was even hurt. She remembered Quinton being inside the vehicle, and he had been until just before the accident. She looked over at me and didn't understand why I didn't go to Kristine; when I did look in her direction, she later told me that I had a blank stare on my face and did not respond. Nellie does remember seeing Quinton's legs behind the Suburban, but thought he was looking under the vehicle for something. She didn't know until much later that Quinton had been called home.

Nellie is an amazingly strong woman, who survived the death of her husband and breast cancer. She stayed with Kristine and, I believe, willed her back from the brink. She implored Kristine not to leave her, even though she was nonresponsive and appeared dead. Before the paramedics arrived, Kristine was showing signs of life. Nellie and some Good Samaritans realized that she was breathing, and her eyes were no longer rolled back into her head.

Quinton's Messages

As Kristine became conscious, she became aware of an intense pressure on her chest and asked Nellie to get off her, but Nellie was not on her and told her so. That was Kristine's first memory as she regained consciousness. We later discovered that Kristine had five broken ribs, along with a broken fibula, serious road rash, and a dangerous blow to the head. Upon regaining consciousness, she immediately tried to get up. Somehow, some way, she knew that other members of her family were in peril, and she was trying to get up. I sat with Quinton and heard a commotion coming from her direction; I remember someone telling her that she could not get up. At that point, they restrained her.

Another Good Samaritan, I believe her name was Sheri, stayed with Quinton and me for much of the time between the accident aftermath and the paramedics' arrival. Sheri was incredible. We hovered over Quinton, exhorting him to wake up. When I realized that his lips were turning blue and his breaths were coming at less frequent intervals, I told her so. I was kind of in limbo, feeling almost as if I was not part of this madness but only observing. Thoughts went rapid-fire through my mind: *Quinton is going to make it* and *No, Quinton isn't going to make it.* All the while none of it really seemed real.

I was focused on Quinton's breathing and blue lips, when Sheri pulled a respiratory kit from her vehicle and, with a declaration of not giving up, went to work on Quinton. We were able to improve his condition only a little—his lips didn't look quite so blue—but there was still no responsiveness in his eyes.

There were paramedics on the scene by then, but they seemed tentative in some way, and from my quite limited perspective, they didn't seem to be taking control of the scene. Maybe that was because they were focused on Kristine, who was still touch and go.

Then Barney Carter arrived and took control of Quinton and me. Barney came to us and gently pulled me away from Quinton to attend to him. He saw what we refused to see. Quinton was already gone, and my precious son's body was experiencing an autonomic reflex as his autonomic nervous system continued to operate, controlling Quinton's involuntary responses. Barney did what he could for Quinton while different paramedics worked on me in an effort to assess my injuries.

I was sitting on the back of the trailer when Barney came to me. The interaction between us seemed more real, more intense than anything else going on around me. There was such emotion in his blue eyes as I asked about my son. All I saw was Barney's eyes. It was as if there was just a pair of blue eyes floating in space, and then he told me that he was not going to lie to me: it didn't look good for Quinton. At that point, I was only beginning to realize that Quinton might be dead. Just before Barney came over, I saw blankets had been placed on Quinton, but my mind was still refusing to accept that he wouldn't make it. I actually thought they were keeping him warm.

Upon discovering that my wonderful son, my pal who had always hung with me was gone, I broke down; it began to sink in. I must have been in shock, because none of it seemed real. The first of many tears washed down my face. I am not one to know emotions, and that was the first time I could remember bawling since I was a child. I stood there bawling while Barney stepped away, and then I began to hyperventilate, but Sheri was there. I wish I knew how to get a hold of her to thank her for being there for us. Sheri was telling me that I had to breathe. I was barely cognizant of her, even though her face was only inches from mine. She kept at it as I began to pass out. I think she started yelling at me to breathe as I told the people around me to either get out of my way because I was going to fall or to catch me, but just before I could pass out I was able to focus on my breathing.

The paramedics gently laid me on the ground as I continued to focus on my breathing. I didn't pass out. They put me on a stretcher and put a brace around my neck as a precaution. Then I instantly changed modes and became focused on everybody else. In a way, I went to work, maybe to insulate myself from the awful grief and sense of loss, to insulate myself from the unbelievable, but also to elude my own emotions once again.

Barney came to me and let me know that Flight for Life was almost there and to cover my eyes. A barrier of paramedics and Good

Samaritans helped block the flying sand. Barney told me that they were undecided on whom to take in Flight for Life, and I gave my two cents as forcefully as I could. I told him to take my wife in the helicopter, because I had non–life-threatening injuries. I seriously doubt that my opinion in the matter made any difference at all, but they loaded Kristine into the helicopter. I directed Barney to have the flight crew take Nellie as well; I could not bear the thought of Kristine being in Farmington, New Mexico (where they would be taking her), all by herself. Barney did what he could, but the helicopter was at its maximum weight with paramedics and emergency gear, so Nellie would have to ride with us in the ambulance to Cortez.

Barney and I were face to face. I implored him to get Nellie and Cheyanne to Farmington, where Kristine would be alone at the San Juan Regional Medical Center. At that point, I really didn't give a damn about myself; I was only thinking of Kristine. In fact, I wanted to be alone to try to make some sense of what had happened. I put every ounce of energy I had into my plea. Barney looked at me and told me that he would get them there, and then he asked if I believed him.

"Yes," I said. "You and I have a connection, and I know you are a good man." Then the conversation was over. I didn't give it another thought. Even then, all I knew of Barney was in his most amazing, intense, and emotional blue eyes. Otherwise, I hadn't a clue what the man looked like.

Into the ambulance we were loaded. Nellie was in the front with Barney; Cheyanne, Layla, and I were in the back. Barney's partner, George, was in the back with us, monitoring me and making sure I didn't hyperventilate again.

Somehow, we had my cell phone, and I asked Cheyanne to call my mom in Virginia. We got her on the line, but because I was lying prone with a neck brace I could not put the phone to my ear, so I spoke into it like a microphone. I remember telling her to listen closely, that there had been an accident, and that we were on the way to the hospital. I tried to be calm and tried to speak slowly, but my mom, Frances Ernell

Jackson, heard the tone of my voice and what wasn't being said. She was frantic when she got off the phone with me, and she immediately called my youngest sister, Regina Jackson, to arrange for a flight west.

Meanwhile, I had one last hope that I might have misread Barney when he had said it didn't look good for Quinton. Maybe that didn't mean he was gone. Maybe he was still fighting for his life, so I asked George. George, bless his soul, was a relatively new paramedic, and that may have been his first call involving the transition of a soul. He indicated that he didn't know, but I was reading his nonverbal expressions and realized that Quinton had left us. I asked Cheyanne to lean close to me, and I whispered in her ear that Quinton hadn't made it.

Barney drove the ambulance and called everyone he knew in the region in an effort to secure rides for Nellie and Cheyanne. Barney, who is now a friend, would not fail. By the time we arrived in Cortez, he had located an off-duty nurse to drive them to Farmington.

Within a week, I began to realize that the accident was the fourth ah-ha moment. This accident was too improbable to be simply chance. Kristine and I survived after being hit by an airborne car going fifty or sixty miles an hour. Quinton wasn't hit by the car and died without suffering. If the accident had happened any other way—if Quinton had suffered or if I could have blamed myself for the accident—I would not have been receptive to what was to come.

Chapter Six

THE HOSPITAL STAY

We arrived at the Cortez Memorial Hospital, and we all went inside to the emergency room—me on a stretcher and everyone else walking. Nellie and Cheyanne were badly shaken as they worried about Kristine.

Just before their ride arrived, Nellie came to me one last time, and I quietly told her, "Nellie, you have to tell Kristine that Quinton didn't make it. She has to know." She didn't want to be the one to tell her, but she reluctantly agreed. From my perspective, not knowing would be worse than knowing.

I turned to Layla and said, "Layla, why don't you go with them? I will be fine here and will find a ride down later."

I don't remember her arguing or what she said, but it was clear that that she intended to stay with me. There was a bond that we had formed at the accident scene, and she refused to leave me alone. Soon, Nellie and Cheyanne were on their way to Farmington to be with Kristine.

The time at Cortez Memorial Hospital wasn't easy. The staff handled me with kid gloves and understandably so. If anyone had snapped a picture of me, I'm certain it would have shown a man with a blank stare and a pained expression on his face. Maybe that was why Layla wouldn't leave me alone. That period of time was the closest I would be to being truly alone over the coming weeks, and it was painful. The reality of Quinton being dead loomed ahead; the reality of Kristine being physically broken and Cheyanne being lost were our immediate focus and somehow more urgent, more pressing than Quinton's death.

My cell phone battery was running down, and I had calls to make. The staff there was on it, and in no time, they gave me a phone charger. A nice nurse indicated that she had another at home and just gave me one. While the phone charged, I sat essentially in silence.

Layla was never far away. I think she only left me once to call her mother, Chris Voldrich. Long afterward, I learned that she had called to tell her mother to get down to Cortez as soon as she could because Quinton had died and she didn't think Kristine would make it. Otherwise, Layla stayed by my side in silence as I grappled with what had happened.

After I set the phone to charge, I had a call come in to the hospital from my sister Regina. I don't remember much of the call; in fact, I initially forgot we had even spoken. Regina reminded me of the gist of the conversation. I let her know that Quinton didn't make it by saying, "My boy is dead. Quinton is dead." I explained that I was in Cortez and expected to be released before the night was over and that Kristine was in Farmington in critical condition with Nellie and Cheyanne on the way there.

While I was in the hospital, they x-rayed my pelvis, hip, and back. Everything was intact, which was another surprise and provided yet another ah-ha moment. It was one of many unexplained events, or events that seemed unexplained at the time, that speak in our minds of a higher power watching over us, even during such a tragedy.

They offered us food. I was more concerned that Layla eat than I eat, but I knew I needed something in order to keep functioning. Layla went with a nurse to the cafeteria to get some food. I can't remember if I was left alone or not, and I can't remember if we spoke at all after the food arrived. I ate all that was in front of me without really tasting it.

After they fed us, I had to go the bathroom, and then I discovered that walking was painful. Something was up with my left foot, so they x-rayed that as well and discovered a small broken bone that didn't need a cast.

After a cursory washing and cleaning of my wounds, they released me. I will never know why they didn't do more with the road rash on my leg; I can only assume that, with so much dirt embedded in my leg, the accepted practice was to let it come to the surface of its own accord. Or maybe I was too anxious to get moving to let them work on me.

Barney arranged a ride for Layla and me to get to Farmington: another off-duty nurse and her daughter took us. We communicated with Cheyanne from the road. We knew that Kristine was stable, that she knew of Quinton's transition, and that she wanted to see me. We later discovered that the nurses and doctors on staff had x-rayed her entire body and she was heavily medicated. She had no recollection of the accident or the helicopter ride.

We arrived at approximately 11:00 p.m. When we arrived, it seem like we had a red carpet laid before us. I imagine that I looked pretty scary with blood and quite a wild eyed expression on my face. If I remember correctly, knowing how I can be at times, I was looking for a fight—something, any sort of a reason to explode, to let it all out. On some level, I was angry about losing my son, and I expect that that anger was in my expression.

Layla and I arrived on the sixth floor to find Nellie and Cheyanne in the intensive care unit (ICU) waiting room. I could feel my anger rising. *Why weren't they with Kristine?* I wondered.

Cheyanne came to me in tears and said, "It was my fault. I wouldn't move my feet, and that was why Quinton stepped out of the Suburban."

I held her tightly as I calmly, lovingly, and intensely told her, "You cannot blame yourself. If you walk around blaming yourself, you won't be able to heal. Don't repeat what you said to me, to anyone. Let it go."

My conversation with Cheyanne was private, and I held her in my arms trying to protect her. I can't remember if Nellie and I spoke.

Immediately afterward, I found myself looking into the ICU and ringing a buzzer for admittance. It was after visiting hours, and I had the impression that I might not be admitted to see Kristine; I was prepared to explode. I had a small bandage on my head and my head wound was still bleeding as the blood seeped out and around the bandage. I was looking for someone to vent my anger at, and this looked like a good opportunity. As I looked in at the staff, I had the impression that they knew who I was. I was let in without comment. Upon my admittance, my angst dissipated quickly behind the walls I had constructed at some point in my life to keep me from feeling pain.

All four of us went into the ICU together, and I did not leave until morning. I don't remember any of the ongoing conversations with anyone at that point other than the conversation with my wife. She was awake and looking at me as if she expected the worst from me. I read in her eyes that she expected me to lash out or to try to cast blame.

"We will only survive this awful nightmare by not blaming others or each other," I gently told her as I held her hand. "We must stand together."

While she has no recollection of this conversation or that I spent the night by her side, I believe the positive energy I brought with me into her room was a turning point in her recovery.

Was this another ah-ha moment? How is it that, with my emotions swinging back and forth between grief, anger, sadness, and hopelessness, impassioned pleas were delivered through me to Cheyanne and Kristine? As I relive that night in 2009, I realize that I wasn't alone. I was being lifted up and held in some way that kept me from losing it completely while that presence used me to deliver a message of hope and love to my family. It is beyond belief, but it is true nevertheless.

The morning of Thursday, June 11 arrived, our first in nine and a half years without Quinton in body. We would soon discover that Quinton was with us in spirit. At six in the morning, I left Kristine and went to the ICU waiting room, where the Cheyanne and Layla were trying to sleep. I lay down with the intent of trying to get some sleep; however, sleep would not come. After I checked on the girls and asked if they had slept, I lay my head down.

As I tried to doze off, I suddenly remembered Quinton at the accident scene. I could not shake the image of the dirt in his braces, his open eyes, and his blank stare. The memory shook me to the core. I couldn't take it. It ripped me apart to see my son like that at the accident scene, and it hurt even more approximately twelve hours later as I tried to sleep.

I got up and started reaching out to my friends and peers. On some level, I knew I needed to do so, but on another level, I understood that I was trying to escape this new reality, to numb the pain.

On my BlackBerry was an e-mail from my friend, Jeff Goldman of Western ProScapes. At the time, he was wishing us a happy vacation. I sent him an e-mail asking him to tell three groups of people what had happened: John and Tracy McDonough, Sandrena Brockman Robinson, and the Denver chapter of the Building Owners and Managers Association office. I apologized for asking him to perform that unpleasant task.

Then I called my friend and fellow Evergreen High School class of '83 graduate, Alex Brister. Alex and I played football against each other while in separate junior high schools and together while attending Evergreen high school. Like many do, we lost contact after we graduated from Evergreen, but we had reconnected in 1999 when I had returned to Conifer after living in Phoenix.

Alex and I had grown close over the years and discovered that we were very similar in emotional makeup. We met two or three times a year, and invariably I would come back to the same refrain: we (our society and I) had lost our spirituality and we were worshiping a false God, money. But we could not get beyond that point. We could not figure out what to do to remedy the problem personally or in terms of our society in this country.

Alex and his wife, Renee, had a son named Garrett fourteen months before Quinton was born. We were only able to make time in our busy schedules a few times to get them together, but they were compatible and enjoyed each other's company. More than that, Quinton and Garrett were very similar to each other just as Alex and I were.

Alex wasn't available, but I spoke to his father, Tom Brister, whom I was also close to and gave him the bad news. I don't think I called anybody else on the morning of the eleventh. Cheyanne was dealing with her grief in much the same way I was dealing with mine, so she had been in contact with her friends from school. The word of our loss spread like wildfire in the Conifer/Evergreen community and among the members of the Denver chapter of the Building Owners and Managers Association (BOMA Denver). My phone blew up with ringing, and I spent the next five days speaking with friends, neighbors, family members, and professional peers as I desperately tried to insulate myself from our new reality.

Before I became completely engrossed in talking and e-mailing, the chaplain came to see Kristine and me in the ICU. Kristine was awake and already getting stronger. She was angry; specifically she was angry with the woman who drove into us and killed our son. Additionally, she wished she had died and not Quinton.

"That woman has to pay for killing our son," she said with venom.

Somehow, I didn't have ill feelings toward Amanda Higgins; in fact, I don't think I ever did. Amanda was twenty-one years old or thereabout. She inexplicably fell asleep while approaching the dirt area where we were parked while not under the influence of any drugs or alcohol and while commuting from college. How could I possibly not feel anger or resentment toward this young woman? Yet I didn't. I saw her at the accident scene when she walked over and realized what she had been a party to. No words were exchanged, but I saw her emotion, and even then I was concerned about her. I believe this to be another example of a presence helping me, standing with me during our worst nightmare.

When the chaplain came in, she comforted Kristine and me, and we both cried like babies. Then we prayed together. I can't remember any other time in my life when I wept uncontrollably like I did that morning. Tears streamed down my face in a torrent, and snot ran from my nose. I held Kristine, and control slowly returned.

In hindsight, this is such an unbelievably important aspect of grieving. We just must find an outlet for all that pain, hurt, shock and even anger if that applies. The weeping is an outlet designed by God for us to purge those emotions. To this day, I look forward to the tears, because I still keep too many of my emotions locked behind a strong veneer.

I paced back and forth all day long and talked to everybody as I tried to balance myself on my crutches while on my BlackBerry. I spent the first day sharing the specifics of what had happened to us. All day long, I paced and talked. I could tell that some of the nurses were getting annoyed with me, but I didn't care. I was busy trying to cope with the loss of my son by *doing*. I couldn't sit still. In my mind, I was communicating, but in reality, I was running as fast as I could, trying to put some distance between me and what I felt. This wasn't a conscious thing, but now I'm clear about what I was doing. By the end of the day, my left leg swelled to twice its normal size because I had refused to stay off it.

During our first full day in the hospital, the chaplain made sleeping arrangements for us at the Marriot Courtyard.

Mike and Chris Voldrich were the first to arrive, and they arrived late that day. They left Conifer immediately upon hearing what had happened. Mike hadn't slept in two days, but he drove the whole way. After arriving completely exhausted, they took me, Cheyanne, and Layla over to our rooms while Nellie stayed with Kristine.

Throughout the day, we had been in contact with my sister, Regina, and my mother. Mom arrived in Las Vegas on a morning flight from Raleigh, North Carolina. Regina picked her up at the airport, and they headed to Farmington in her car. We were anxious to see them and they to see us. Cheyanne and Regina were pretty close. Cheyanne was on the phone with Regina all through the day and into the evening as she charted their progress. It seemed like it took them forever.

At one point, I overheard Cheyanne on the phone with Regina, imploring her to get to us as soon as she could. I called Regina back, gently telling her, "Please drive safely. Don't take any chances, and watch for people walking on the road. We don't need you to get into an accident while trying to get to us."

They finally arrived around midnight.

However, before they arrived, Uncle Jim and Aunt Troy arrived around 11:00 p.m. They drove in from Phoenix. They stopped by the hospital to see Nellie and Kristine and then came to the Marriott. We visited briefly, and they retired to their rooms.

When my mother, Regina, and Regina's boyfriend, Jeff, arrived, they came straight to our room. They immediately went to work on my wounds. The worst was the road rash on my left leg and both feet. There was still a lot of dirt and gravel embedded in me. I had been so busy pacing and talking on the phone that I had neglected myself. Within an hour, they had me cleaned up with fresh bandages and in bed with ice on my swollen leg. The swelling was between my knee and ankle, and that area was truly double its normal size.

At that point, I hadn't slept in thirty-six hours, and I still hadn't filled the pain prescriptions given to me at the Cortez hospital. Subsequently, I slept fitfully until the morning.

This is a good point in the telling of our story to share the perspectives of my mom and sister.

My Mom's Perspective

My mom, Frances Jackson, wrote, "On or about 8:30 p.m. Eastern Standard Time, I received a call from my son, Ernie, who informed me that there had been an accident. He told me he was in an ambulance headed to the hospital and that Kristine was being sent by helicopter to Farmington, New Mexico. He told me Cheyanne was fine and that he did not think Quinton made it. I knew by the tone of his voice that Quinton was gone. I didn't want to believe Quinton was gone, but in my heart I knew. I talked to Nellie and Cheyanne (on Cheyanne's cell phone). They did not know where Quinton was, and then I knew for sure. What a gut-wrenching feeling, knowing my son and family were suffering while I was so far away and could not be there for them. It hurt so badly that I cannot describe the pain.

"Within an hour, I had a ticket to Nevada (where my youngest daughter, Regina, lives). The next morning, I left on my way to be with Ernie, Kristine, Cheyanne, and Nellie. Regina and Jeff picked me up at the Las Vegas airport, and we drove to New Mexico, where everybody was. What a ride trying to get there quickly while trying to be careful in the process. Our emotions were all over the place. When we arrived and found Ernie in the hotel room alone, trying to take care of his wounded leg, I almost lost it. It was like seeing your baby all alone. Jeff and Regina went out to get medical supplies. When they returned, they cleaned and bandaged his leg. He was so grateful.

"The next morning, we got to see Kristine in the hospital. I was not prepared for what I saw. She was badly injured—another gut-wrenching moment. It was a rough week trying to get Ernie and Kristine well enough to get home. So many emotions . . . but Ernie and Kristine were so strong. I do not know how they did it knowing Quinton was gone. We all held it together the best we could. Nellie was a great comfort for me; she is so strong. I know we were all in shock."

Regina's Perspective

"It started out as a normal day. I went to work, and Jeff had an appointment for his knee. We left the doctor, got something to eat, and came home. I was tired; I was going to take a short nap before picking up the girls from Pete's (my former husband and the father of my twins).

"The phone rang. It was Mom, and I will never forget that phone call: 'Regina! There's been an accident; it's Ernie, and he doesn't think Quinton made it.'

"The desperation in Mom's voice rocked my core. This couldn't be. Maybe I had fallen asleep, and this was a bad dream. I immediately wanted to know where they were. I put my shoes on and was leaving for . . . I don't know where, but I was going. Mom told me to slow down.

"'We need to get information before we jump in the car.'

"'Okay, I'll wait but not for long.'

"Mom told me Ernie had called from the ambulance and that Kristine was hurt too. I wondered what the hell had happened. I needed to get to them. Mom said she would call me back when she heard something, so I waited and waited for what felt like hours, but it was actually only minutes. *How could this be happening? What is happening?* I grew increasingly impatient and called Mom back; she was very upset and hadn't heard any more news.

"I began to get frantic. I needed to get to Ernie, Kristine, and the kids. I needed to find out where they were so we could go . . . right then. Jeff suggested I call the highway patrol to get some information, so I made the call to Colorado Highway Patrol. They were aware of the accident, but they did not have any details. They forwarded me to the Towaoc Police who handled the accident, and they too did not have any details. That time, I was forwarded to the hospital in Cortez. The emergency room attendant picked up the phone, and I could feel my heart racing, and my stomach felt like it was turning flips. I quickly explained why I was calling and was told that no information could be given over the phone. They were not completely sure I was family.

"At that point, I reached a level of sheer panic. I don't remember what I said, but I remember thinking that my brother was there and they wouldn't even tell me if he was okay. Whatever I said, the lady asked me to hold for what felt like an eternity. My heart was pounding, my ears were ringing, and I was scared, so scared. Then Ernie was on the line.

Quinton's Messages

"'Hello?'"

"'Ernie?' I said.

"'Who is this?" he asked.

"'Your sister,' I said. 'What happened?'

"I will never forget his next words: 'My boy is gone. My boy is dead. My boy is dead.'

"'Are you sure?' I asked like a stupid ass. Like he wouldn't know. I just didn't want it to be true, not Quinton, not Ernie. *Oh my God.* My mind raced. *Cheyanne? Kristine?*

"Ernie briefly filled me in as to everyone's locations, and I assured him that we were on our way; we would wait for Mom, and we would be on our way. I told Ernie I loved him, and then I fell apart after hanging up the phone.

"I had to get there, no matter what. I needed to be there. Ernie needed us.

"I called Mom and confirmed the worst: Quinton was indeed gone. I couldn't think straight. I felt like someone or something had reached in and torn out a piece of my heart. It hurt so badly; it was indescribable.

"Then I had to think about Mom, get her to Vegas, and then drive . . . to where? By then, Ernie would know where we needed to go, whether it was Cortez, Colorado, or Farmington, New Mexico. I was immediately online looking for airfare for Mom; luckily, there was an early flight that could get her here by 10:00 a.m. the next morning.

"*Okay,* I thought, *now I can make arrangements for the kids. Wow, my girls. How are they going to handle this?* I couldn't tell them and leave it at that; we would tell them when we got back. I didn't want to take them. They did not need to experience this at that point in their lives, not yet.

"I was numb. I called Cheyanne, and she was hysterical. There was no calming her. I told her I was coming, and she begged me to hurry. I couldn't get there fast enough, and I was not even sure where *there* was, but I would get there.

"I felt like someone had sucked the life out of me, but I packed my children, made calls, made plans. By 10:00 p.m. everything was set, and the kids would be taken care of. Mom would soon be on her way, and then we would be on our way.

"I needed rest; we had a long drive the next day. I was tired, but I couldn't sleep. My mind was racing. My heart was racing. Eventually, I fell asleep for about an hour, and then I was awake, watching the clock. Mom should have been on her way to the airport by then. She would be here soon, and we would go. I begged for sleep, but it didn't come. I couldn't get the situation out of my head. I couldn't stop thinking about Ernie and everybody. *Quinton . . . where is he? Is he alone? Is he okay? I don't want him to be lost; he needs to find his way to his mom, dad, and sister.* I finally fell asleep, and then the alarm went off.

"I got up, put gas in the Hummer, fed the dogs, and went to get Mom. Her flight was on time. Mom and I hugged and cried; we were both still in shock that it was even happening. My stomach was in knots. Mom looked so sad and fragile; I needed to make sure she was okay throughout this. She looked lost. I felt lost and empty, but my goal was to go until we got there.

"We were on our way to Farmington, New Mexico, where Kristine was in the hospital. Ernie had arrived in Farmington during the evening and was now there with Cheyanne, Nellie, and Layla. We were driving. We had movies for Mom to watch in an attempt to occupy her time. Traffic sucked. The Hoover Dam was under construction; there were massive delays. It was insane. I needed to get somewhere.

"Cheyanne called and wanted to know how far away we were. I told her we were just in Arizona but that we were coming as fast as we could. She said they needed clothes and toiletries; everything they had had been left in their Suburban. We stopped in Kingman and went to Wal-Mart. I couldn't think. I was grabbing what I could, but I wanted to be on the road. Clothing, toothbrushes—whatever they might have needed I grabbed.

"We stopped to eat. I didn't want to, but Jeff insisted, because he knew we needed our strength. But if I didn't get back on the road soon, I was going to have a conniption fit. That day was taking so long, and we weren't even close to reaching them yet. I couldn't stop thinking that we needed to get there; it was making me crazy.

"When we were back on the road, I was driving and hauling ass, but I needed to be careful. I tried to slow down, but my speed eventually went back up. In Flagstaff, we gassed up and went; it was time to cross the desert. We were making good time.

"I put the movie *Benjamin Button* on for Mom in an attempt to distract her from what was to come. I was driving and listening to the movie. There was a scene in the movie in which one of the characters was hit by a car, and a sequence of events was shown that led to the exact moment that had changed her life forever. One insignificant tiny event had changed an entire sequence of events. What was that life-altering event that led to the accident at that exact moment and place?

"My mind raced again. Maybe the other driver stopped for coffee or to use the bathroom or left early or late—anything could have put her in that exact spot at that exact time while Ernie was there. Maybe Ernie and Kristine stopped for coffee or stopped for a bathroom break or left early or left late. I was going to make myself crazy thinking like that, but I wanted to know. I couldn't change it, but I wanted to know.

"While we were still driving, I wondered, *Why did this have to happen? I never want Ernie to hurt; it hurts to my core knowing the pain he is going through. He has already endured so much pain, much more than most.* There was that feeling again that someone had ripped my heart out. I felt like I was going to be sick, and the tears burned my eyes.

"Cheyanne called, and there was desperation in her voice.

"'Where are you? Please hurry!'

"'I am, sweetheart. We are coming. We will be there,' I said.

"Then Ernie called and said, 'Be careful. Slow down, and be safe.'

"That was really hard to do, but I tried. How was he able to worry about us when his world had been turned upside down?

"It was starting to get dark, and we were approaching the turnoff for Four Corners. We were close to where it happened. *Oh my God*! My stomach dropped. *Is Quinton lost out here?* I didn't know; I just wanted a sign. I was sure he had found his way to his mom and dad. I was watching for any sign. For a sign of what I didn't know, just a sign.

"The road went on forever. *Is it never going to end? Are we ever going to get there?* I needed to see Ernie; I needed to see if he was okay.

"Mom was tired. She looked broken. I hadn't seen that look since I was a kid. I needed to make sure she got some rest.

"Finally, we were there after what felt like an eternity. The lights of Farmington were in view. I was nervous, and I was sad. I didn't know what to expect. We finally arrived at the hotel after getting lost in Farmington, and it was too late to go to the hospital, so we went straight to the hotel where Ernie was.

"My stomach was burning, and my eyes were hot with tears as we walked into the building, headed to the elevator and went up to Ernie's floor. We knocked on the door, and after what felt like forever, Ernie opened it. I will never forget that look, that pained expression; I had seen it before, but that time it was different. That image has been permanently seared into my brain. I will never forget. There was that feeling again too, like someone had reached in and torn out another piece of me. I wanted to take his pain, to take it all away. It was not fair, not fair at all. I felt like the ground was being yanked out from under my feet. *Stay strong, Regina*, I thought. *Ernie needs you.*

"Ernie sat down, and I looked at his wounds. He was a mess. There was dirt in his leg and dirt in his head. I was pissed off. Why hadn't they cleaned him up? I was shaking and fighting the tears. He was so hurt physically and emotionally. I wanted to take it all away, but I didn't know how. I hugged him and held his hand.

"He needed to get those wounds cleaned or he would get an infection. Jeff and I headed out to find a Walgreens or a Wal-Mart or whatever would open in the middle of the night. We bought bandages, peroxide, betadine, and anything that would help.

"I wondered how Kristine was feeling. Was she awake? Was she in pain? I wanted to see Cheyanne, to hug her, to make her feel better, although I was not sure that was possible.

"When we got back to the hotel, Jeff cleaned Ernie's wounds, and I held his hand. I couldn't believe this was happening, but it was. This was really happening. I felt like we were in slow motion. I wanted to scream, to cry, and to yell, 'Why?' I was angry, so angry. *Why?*

"It was too late to see Cheyanne and Kristine that night—Cheyanne was at the hospital with her mom—so we went to our room, and I hoped for sleep, but every time I closed my eyes, I saw Quinton's face; I saw Ernie's face when he opened the hotel room door. I couldn't sleep. I was very uneasy. *Where is Quinton? Is he alone?* I wondered. I couldn't stop those thoughts.

"The next morning, Cheyanne came back from the hospital. She was so sad and looked so lost. We were going to go to Cortez to clean out their vehicle, and Cheyanne wanted to go, but all of us told her she needed to stay and get some rest. I promised her I would get Quinton's things and I would look for his rocks (which he had collected while on vacation). It was going to be hard, but I was going. I was doing it for Ernie, and it was at his request that Jeff, Mike Voldrich, and I prepared to leave. No one else was going to rifle through their things without one of us there. I would go, but I was scared.

"We drove out and looked for the turnoff to Cortez. I knew it was there, but we hadn't come up on it yet. *What the hell? I saw it last night on our way into Farmington,* I thought. I soon realized that we had missed the turnoff and were going to drive past the scene of the accident. I was scared, but I wanted to see. We made the turn down Highway 160, and I looked for mile marker one, and then we saw the large pullout area. Jeff pulled in, and we got out.

"We really weren't sure if we were in the right spot, and then we spotted the tire tracks going off the hill and started to walk around. I saw orange paint marking where tires had been, and then I knew we were at the spot. The paint marked where the Suburban had been parked with the trailer in tow. There was a shoe that was one of Ernie's sandals. Just next to that was a small flip-flop turned and bent in half. Quinton's. Tears started to burn. That was it; there was no doubt.

"I felt the air being sucked out of my lungs. Everything was in slow motion. I turned and looked around, and it all came into focus. I could see the Suburban and the trailer, Ernie, and Quinton. I could see them like I was there. I wanted to scream, to tell them to move. Why didn't they move? They couldn't hear me. It was like I was watching through a screen, and no one could hear or see me. The swirling chaos—I could see it all, and then it was over.

"Then I was standing there, crying, screaming, 'Why? Why? Why?' I looked at the shoes, and then I saw it: the blood on a rock, so much blood. Quinton was right there. I couldn't believe it was happening. I tried to find where Kristine was, but I couldn't find a clear sign. She must have been near the tire tracks going haphazardly off the embankment. I couldn't believe I was standing there at the exact spot where all our lives had been changed forever in that single moment in time; there was no going back.

"We got back in our truck and headed toward Cortez. I didn't want to leave though, as though staying there would make it go away. I felt like I needed to see some sign that Quinton was okay; I didn't know why I thought it would be there.

"On the way to Cortez, I realized that I was scared to see what the Suburban looked like, although Ernie didn't think it had any damage at all. As we got closer, we were not sure where we were supposed to go, but Jeff figured it out. We pulled up to a lot that was supposed to be it. I didn't see much until we turned the last corner to the gate, and then there it was. Through the fence, I could see the Suburban at the back of the lot. It was backed in, and next to it was what I assumed to be the trailer; it was backed in as well, and I saw two Jet Skis on it. My stomach dropped. I started to shake again.

"Someone walked up to open the gate and asked who we were. We told him and had to call Ernie so he could verify that we were the ones who were allowed to be there to clean out the truck. After the phone call, we were allowed in. Jeff drove to the back and pulled up next to the Suburban.

"We pulled up on the passenger side, and I was shocked by how badly damaged it was. The front door was held closed by a seatbelt wrapped through the window and the window of the back passenger door. The front door wouldn't close completely on its own, and the entire side of the truck was badly dented. I felt sick. I wanted to throw up. And that idiot's bumper was in Ernie's backseat. The truck was a mess, much worse than I ever expected. I got out and stood there in shock. I didn't know what to think. I was looking at Ernie's truck, Quinton's last moments, the pain . . . I needed to throw up. Everything was swirling. I couldn't breathe. Someone was sucking the air out of my lungs."

My sister's writing is so different from mine. Within her text, I can feel the angst and the raw emotion that mine only hints at.

Chapter Seven

THE WEEK OF JUNE 12

Friday, June 12 through Monday, June 15 was a blur. Having our families and the Voldrichs there was just what we needed to get us through. In addition, some friends showed why they were friends, and some acquaintances became friends.

On June 12, Uncle Jim filled my prescriptions, which included one for pain medication. It was the night of the twelfth that I first took a pain pill and a muscle relaxant to ensure that I would receive a decent night of sleep. I turned the light out that night and lay there in bed. As I lay there, I began to drift off to sleep, I felt my left hand being held. It was so comforting, so I surmised that, somehow, that sensation was because of all the prayers being directed our way. You see, at that point, I still didn't understand what was possible. While I was still down in Farmington, I noted that the prayers were continuing, but I didn't experience that sensation again. It was only then that I realized that Quinton had been holding my hand. But even then I still didn't completely understand the significance of the event.

Kristine's recovery was nothing short of miraculous. She continued to get stronger and stronger. On June 10 at five fifty, she was essentially dead, but by Saturday, June 13, the staff at San Juan Medical Center was making preparations to move her out of ICU and into her own room on the third floor. Kristine was still in a lot of pain, especially from her ribs, but she also had blurred vision from the blow she had taken above her right eye. In fact, her right eye had blood in it. In addition, her hands were badly bruised and swollen, and she had open wounds on her back where flesh had been ripped away. While she had improved and was stable, she was in a lot of pain and subsequently slept a lot while in ICU.

Our families kept our spirits up, especially for the girls. Cheyanne was hurting, but she continued to keep up a brave front. I was always on the phone. So many of our friends and the people we knew sent e-mails and reached out to us while we were in Farmington. All the while, God was preparing to use me and my friend John McDonough as conduits for messages.

On June 13, I felt the need to write. When I sat down, I just wrote without purpose or reason other than to express some of what I was feeling. In the notebook that I brought with me on vacation for the express purpose of receiving a message, I wrote:

> Our son, Quinton Stone Jackson, died in a freak accident at approximately 5:45 p.m. on Wednesday, June 10. Quinton died helping his father, which is no surprise, if you know Quinton.
>
> Quinton was an angel walking among us, whom we were blessed to have in our lives for nine and a half years. He had the kindest soul and the most loving heart, and all he wanted to do was help. If anybody was down or in need, Quinton was there whether that person was a friend, a fellow student, or a family member.
>
> Quinton is survived by his sister, Cheyanne, his mother, Kristine, his father, Ernie, his grandmothers, Nellie and Frances, and a multitude of cousins, aunts, uncles, and friends.
>
> In this dark time while we take solace in the fact that Quinton did not suffer, we must strive to live our individual lives in a way that honors Quinton (e.g., walk in love and kindness and help everyone in need). For parents reading this, love your children every minute of every day. Squeeze them and hold them tenderly. Do it for Quinton and his surviving family.

Quinton's Messages

I do not believe I wrote that alone. As I worked on the book on March 24, 2010, it seemed even more difficult to believe that the above was written without purpose on my part. On the other hand, of course it was written without purpose on my part. That is part of the message we are here to share. Indeed, I had help writing it from God above; that is the only explanation, and it continued. Maybe the help I had was what some call the Holy Spirit.

About the same time as I wrote the above in the notebook, I received an e-mail from John McDonough on my BlackBerry with the following message:

In an instant,
In the beat of a hummingbird's wing,
Faster than the blink of an eye . . .
. . . nothing will ever be the same.
There is only before and after
that moment in time.
Before is a gift that no one can steal;
After is a choice, a story yet to be written.
To not create a beautiful tomorrow
would be like throwing away
all of the yesterdays.
Today, I cannot see that future;
the dark clouds that surround
yet comfort me
block out that sky,
that rainbow after the storm,
beaconing me toward tomorrow.

John indicated that he also didn't write that alone. He later shared with us that these messages sometimes come to him in moments of tragedy. I have known John since 1998; first he was my mentor in the Building Owners and Managers Association, and soon afterward, he was a friend. For years I have felt a special affinity for both John and his wife, Tracey. Maybe on some level we knew this moment was coming and that we would experience it together. His e-mail ended up being the message on the prayer cards we distributed at the service.

During the process of writing this book, I provided John with a copy of a rough manuscript to review. After reviewing it, John wrote:

> I'll never forget the gut shot that I felt when hearing the news. Ernie and I . . . we're never buddy-buddy, but we had a bond, a connection. We met through a trade association and immediately clicked. Every interaction we had reinforced my respect and admiration for him. And over the years, seeing his love for his family, experiencing his connection with his only son, the last time just a week or two earlier—all hit me, because I knew what had just happened. I could not imagine what he and Kristine must be going through. I was hundreds of miles away and unable to reach out to help a friend in need. What could I do? What could anyone *say* that might help?
>
> I always fancied myself a bit of a wordsmith, and I had written many things over the years that I have been proud of. A few times in previous moments of personal pain, I found words flowing from me that put on paper feelings I had no voice to speak. Words poured out on paper along with my tears.
>
> Only a handful of hours after hearing the news, I experienced just such a moment and found a few words that I hoped could break through to someone experiencing a loss beyond my ability to fathom. I cannot put into words the joy of knowing that these simple words, words that came to me so easily, gave some small measure of comfort to my dear friends and have since touched so many.

A lot was going on during this period of time. The community dove into an effort to share information and prepare a fabric of support for our return. Our neighbors and friends showed that they were angels. God directed and empowered several to act as angels over the next weeks. When the community found out, Katherine and Collin Price spearheaded the establishment of a community web page for us on the lotsahelpinghands network. Katherine set up the page, and she and Cathie Nicholson were its administrators.

Meanwhile, Alex Brister and I were speaking several times a day. He shared information with the network of Evergreen High School graduates, which included Jenifer Mintle, who maintains contact with many of the graduates from the early eighties. As I became aware of the massive efforts on our behalf, I coordinated a meeting with Cathie Nicholson and Alex Brister, so he could also be a coordinator on the lotsahelpinghands network.

Kristine and I met Cathie and Troy Nicholson not long after we moved to Conifer in 1998. Cheyanne and their daughter, Megan, became the best of friends while in elementary school. Megan spent a lot of time at our home watching movies and having dinner with us. Quinton was born three years ahead of their son, Ryan, and they became close as well. The girls weren't as close in middle school and high school, and for that matter, we adults spent less time together as years passed, but when we did visit, it was always enjoyable.

Sally and John Lapham were also in the mix of coordinating the community efforts. Sally had embraced us first when we first arrived in Conifer. She had always been there for us; in fact, she and her husband watched Cheyanne while Kristine delivered Quinton.

As time progressed, I spent time speaking with Alex, Cathie, and Sally. I provided them with updates of Kristine's condition, and they in turn updated the community network with the most current information. For a short time, BOMA Denver was not aware of the community network, but that was remedied after I coordinated a phone meeting between Alex Brister and Jeannie Bernard, BOMA Denver's executive director. We also plugged my then employer, Schnitzer West, into the site through my conversations with my immediate supervisor, Lynda Collie. The network eventually drew more than four hundred members, who received updates about our condition as soon as information became available. Both Katherine and Cathie were amazed by how quickly our site grew to so many members; together they approved new member requests as fast as they could.

On Sunday, June 14, Kristine was released from the ICU and moved to a private room on the third floor. When the morning dawned, Mike Voldrich took me back to Kristine's side. While Chris, Layla, and I waited in the lobby, I was using my BlackBerry at a feverish pace. I alternated between checking e-mail and talking to Alex, who was coordinating our trip home. I mean, I was entirely focused on the task at hand and on avoiding my own emotions. In hindsight, I think I was unapproachable.

Mike arrived with his car and picked me up. The entire family, including Uncle Jim, was still there and was returning to the hospital as well. In my opinion, Uncle Jim became the new family patriarch after Ed passed away in 2003. He was wise and kind and showed his experience in these matters. He kept the banter light-hearted, and I was astonished that we were smiling and joking in the room. Sure enough though, the moment the smiling and bantering grew silent, the tears came. In the afternoon, the mood was really somber. The silence became noticeable, and I started to despair. *How could this be?* I found myself staring off into the distance, thinking of Quinton alone somewhere in the dark. I could easily have begun spiraling out of control into a dark abyss, but then at that exact moment, Chris and Layla Voldrich arrived from the Marriot Courtyard.

When Chris arrived, she noticed that not everyone was present.

"I have something to share, and I think I can only share it once," she said.

She was visibly excited and was almost bouncing off the ceiling. Some of us mistook her excitement as despair and became concerned that something else horrible might have happened. Soon, the whole support group was assembled.

"A medicine man in full gear walked up to us in the Marriot Courtyard lobby after you left, Ernie," she started. "When he reached us he gently reached for my hands, and while looking deeply into my eyes, he said, 'I just finished performing a ceremony and was sent to find you.'" Chris paused; she had our attention. We really didn't know what to expect and suspense filled the room. She continued, "The medicine man said, 'The little boy wants you to know that he is fine.'"

We collectively gasped, and many of us began to cry. There was no coincidence that the message came at the exact moment of my despair. Chris continued, telling us that the medicine man added that Quinton was in a better place, that Tom was helping him with his transition, and Tom would be helping Kristine and me at some point.

Chris was forced to pause again, as all of us looked around and asked, "Who is Tom?" Chris didn't know, and neither did we. To this day we are still puzzled about Tom and how he will be helping us.. Then her message took an unexpected twist.

Chris continued, "The Medicine Man said, 'The insurance claim/lawsuit will take longer than expected but will work out well in the end.'"

We were beside ourselves with excitement when she finished—a message from our deceased son, from a place of pure energy (that being spirit).

At that point, just knowing that Quinton was fine was what we needed to hear. Very quickly, I realized that, because our son was able to get a message to us, there is more to our existence than these bags of bones in which we currently reside. That realization has given my life a different direction and a new purpose.

In subsequent conversations with me, Chris shared that the medicine man's presence was captivating. She could feel his energy in his touch and see it in his eyes. After he turned to leave the hotel lobby, Chris and Layla turned to each other and asked, "Did that really happen?" When they turned around again, he was gone.

That was the first of many messages, but I was still a little skeptical because I didn't understand why the medicine man was there to begin with.

During the week of June 22, after Quinton's service, I couldn't sleep.

Subsequently, I woke up and decided to try to find out why the medicine man had been there in the Marriot Courtyard lobby in full gear. I went to our computer and searched for "Medicine Men." After an hour and a half, I learned some very interesting information. For example, in South Dakota, there is a hospital with a medicine man on staff to help heal patients. *Wow,* I thought. That was amazing, but it was not exactly what I was looking for. I knew my search was way too broad. I typed in what I thought was nonsensical—"Four Corners Medicine Men"—and found the answer to my question. In *The Daily Times* of Farmington, New Mexico, and the Cortez, Colorado paper, *The Cortez Journal*, the following article appeared on June 17.

> WINDOW ROCK, Arizona—As many as 250 medicine men from North and South America will gather in Window Rock, Arizona, starting Thursday [June 18], for the 60ᵗʰ annual conference of the Native American Church of North America.
>
> The Native American Church uses peyote to allow Communion with God and to give healing.
>
> But medicine men find the practice is becoming more complex as laws governing the use of feathers, herbs, and plants become stricter.
>
> The president of the Arizona chapter of the Native American Church, Emerson Jackson, says federal representatives will talk with attendees about the rules governing what medicine men use, including eagle feathers, plants, and herbs.
>
> The event, which runs through Sunday, also includes religious ceremonies and a sweat lodge.

Reading this article lifted a load off my shoulders. Once I understood why the medicine man was there, it removed the last bit of doubt I had. Okay, then I could understand and could accept that Quinton had indeed sent a message to us.

All the while, our activity and that of the community was increasing. In conversations with Alex Brister, I discussed the possibility of an obituary in the *Canyon Courier* and *High Timber Times*, two local papers that served the Evergreen and Conifer areas. I can't remember who brought up the topic—probably Alex and his wife, Renee—but I was eager to make it happen. During the discussion, I let them know that I had written something that would probably be a perfect obituary. I faxed it to Alex's home office and to Sally Lapham. Next, we needed a picture of Quinton for the papers. Kristine had current pictures in her purse, and we chose a 2008–2009 picture of Quinton with a vibrant green background, because it reminded us of Quinton's love of nature. The picture was scanned and e-mailed to Alex and Sally with the assistance of the hospital staff. The deadline to get the obituary and picture in was Tuesday, June 16, but before we could finalize the column, we needed to schedule Quinton's service.

2008-09

Quinton's 2008–2009 class picture

Kristine is a lifelong Catholic, and she was very clear about wanting the service held at Our Lady of the Pines in Conifer. We hadn't been to church in some time, so there was a concern about whether or not a service there was possible. As quickly as that, Joanne Rodriguez inquired with our neighbors, George and Mary Linehan, who were well connected with the church. George and Mary vouched for our character, and the service was scheduled for Friday, June 19. That information was subsequently included in the obituary.

The love and support from our family and friends who were on-site in Farmington with us was amazing. Mike Voldrich showed up on the eleventh after not sleeping for forty-eight hours. He arrived and didn't know what to do with himself. I implored him to sleep and told him that we were just happy he was there. He felt like a fifth wheel as our families arrived, but fortunately, he stayed and ended up playing an integral role in our welfare. And Layla continued to astound everyone. She was our primary caregiver beyond the hospital staff. She insisted doing whatever was needed to be done. Her singular focus was incredible. Layla was so intent on her caregiving that none of us would dare dissuade her, even if we wanted to. What an amazing young lady!

The coordinators of the family's lotsahelpinghands site discussed among themselves the need to set up a memorial fund in Quinton's honor. For some reason, I wasn't very receptive; I replied, "Cathie, this isn't about money. Times are tough out there during this recession, and I don't want people feeling obligated to send money to us." I was firm with Cathie, but then Alex called to explain the rationale. Alex made it clear that people loved and respected the entire family and wanted to help. I relented, and Alex established the Quinton Stone Jackson Memorial Fund at the Conifer branch of Bank of the West. All of the information was included in the obituary and submitted to the newspapers, which went out on Thursday, June 18. The information was also circulated as soon as the information became available on Tuesday, June 16, via the helping hands page and BOMA Denver.

We still didn't know specifically when we would be going home to

Conifer. Several friends, including Alex Brister and Tony Rodriguez, offered to drive down to Farmington to pick us up and drive us home. Meanwhile, my friends and former teammates from Evergreen High School, Alex, Bob Pieper, and Doug Wills discussed getting us home. Doug was concerned about us being submitted to an eight-hour drive after all that we had been through. I didn't care; I just wanted to get us home.

While Doug, Bob, and Alex discussed options for getting us home once Kristine was released, I worked with my employer at the time, Schnitzer West, who had an insurance policy that would make the arrangements and cover the expense for their employees to get home in the event of an accident such as ours. However, once the arrangements were close to being made through my employer's program, we were already home. Doug arranged a flight on a single-engine, six-seat Piper for all of us, including my mom, but unfortunately, we didn't have room for Layla, who ended up driving home with her parents.

Kathryn Price, Cathie Nicholson, and Sally Lapham worked feverishly on the helping hands network and with the community to organize the outpouring of support. Sally and her husband, Jon, brought their pop-up camper to our home just in case we ran out of room for family sleeping arrangements. Sally also cleaned our home—not that it was dirty—and she commented to Cathie, "You know how Ernie is," referring to the fact that I can be something of a neat freak.

It also seemed that the entire communities of Conifer, Evergreen, and BOMA Denver wanted to bring us prepared dinners. We would not have room for them if they all came at once. In one of my conversations—yes, I was still on the phone in an attempt to hide from the awful tragedy—I expressed this concern. I had cut my teeth in commercial real estate at Plaza Tower One, where I had worked for six and a half years. I was on the phone with Robert Aguilar from Plaza Tower One when I mentioned we might have to deal with an excess of food when we arrived home. Robert then spoke with Dan Simpson, the general manager of the building. The staff and many of the tenants pitched in for a free-standing, full-size freezer, which was delivered by Robert after we arrived back in Conifer. Meanwhile, dinners were scheduled through the end of July.

This outpouring of support and love still overwhelms us. Such love was directed toward us, toward all of us. Not only had Quinton made a difference in so many people's lives, but so had Kristine, Cheyanne, and I. As time passed, we heard story after story about how Quinton had impacted the community in ways unbeknownst to us.

Chapter Eight

GOING HOME

We still didn't know specifically when Kristine would be released. We knew it would be during the week of the fifteenth, but that was all we knew. Sometime on Sunday, June 14, I pointedly asked one of Kristine's doctors when we could leave, and I was very direct about my intention of leaving as soon as possible. I was surprised by the response I received; he said it was fine.

I relayed the information to Alex to set it up. Doug had his flying license, but he was unable to break away; he spoke with his instructor, Bob Stedman, and the flight was tentatively scheduled for either late Monday or early Tuesday out of the local airport in Farmington, New Mexico. After checking the weather forecast, Bob recommended that we leave Tuesday morning to avoid the anticipated afternoon thunderstorms that were common in the Rocky Mountain region.

With a firm date and relatively firm time for our arrival in Conifer, the community prepared to welcome us with open arms. As with so many situations when there are a lot of strong people involved with a common goal, disagreements occurred. Our immediate neighbors planned on greeting us at our home when we arrived, which can produce a delicate situation, because one never really knows how people grieve and the intensity of the emotions being felt. There was a concern that too many people might be present. The concern was valid, but I could not bear the thought of coming home to an empty house without our son. I *needed* my friends there. The despair was lurking ever closer to the surface, and it scared me. I was afraid of the silence, afraid of the pain and anguish over what had happened that was lurking just below the surface.

The rest of our family had to get back to their lives and left earlier in the week. Uncle Jim and Aunt Troy left Monday as did my sister and her boyfriend. They had kept us afloat emotionally and physically in our darkest moments.

The morning of Tuesday, June 16 arrived. Mike Voldrich took us to the airport in Farmington, New Mexico. My mom stayed with us on our trip home to Conifer.

We were still beat up; in fact, Bob Stedman later commented to Doug Wills and Alex Brister, "I was not prepared for what I saw when they arrived at the airport." I was on crutches with scabs on my forehead, arms, and legs. Kristine was in a wheelchair and probably should not have been flying; one of the final questions in preparation for the flight home was whether or not Kristine would be capable of sitting in a chair or whether she would require a stretcher. Between Doug, Alex, Bob, and me, we decided to take the cautious route and had the plane equipped with a stretcher. The consensus was that it would be better to have a stretcher and not need it than to not have a stretcher and need it. It was a good decision; Kristine would not have been able to endure the flight any other way.

But, because we had a stretcher for Kristine, we only had room for five and were unable to include Layla on the flight. It broke my heart not to include her after all she had done for us on the vacation, at the accident scene, and at the hospital.

When we left, I sat up front in the copilot seat with Bob; Kristine, Cheyanne, Nellie, and Frances were behind me. The weather was beautiful, and turbulence was minimal, but it was our first time in a small plane. The flight to Centennial airport took a little over an hour; that hour of relative silence and not being on the phone let emotions bubble a little closer to the surface.

The days had passed in a blur for me in a whirlwind of activity. I hadn't taken time to feel, reflect, or grieve. My focus, on the surface anyway, was on getting us home. I really didn't know what I expected to find once we made it home—maybe a sense of normalcy or a sanctuary. On a deeper level, it was clear that I was trying not to feel anything—no pain, no anger, no sadness, no grief. For the most part, I had succeeded.

I cried as we flew over the San Juan Mountains; I realized that Quinton would have loved the view, but he wouldn't get a chance to see it. As I had that thought and shared it with the others on the plane, I realized he was seeing it with us.

When we landed at the Centennial regional airport without incident, Alex and Renee Brister were there waiting for us. Bob Stedman taxied the airplane to the appropriate hanger, and then Bob and Alex helped us offload. It was an emotional time and one of many yet to come. None of us really knew what to say, but within this unfamiliar territory, Renee and Alex were doing everything they could possibly do to keep us comfortable.

We went home in separate cars; Mom went with Renee, and the rest of us went with Alex in his Dodge Caravan. Alex continued to coordinate information for distribution to everyone, reaching out on his cell phone to tell the community that we were on the ground.

"Kristine, are you hungry?" I remember asking. "Do you want us to stop along the way?"

"No, I just want to be home," she said.

We arrived home around noon without our son. I can't tell you how tough it was to pull up to our home and walk inside without Quinton. We were not prepared for that moment. Climbing out of the vehicle, I felt as if we were moving in slow motion. Time had slowed in some way. Reality had changed, and we were all lost, struggling to find our footing. We slowly entered our home, which no longer felt the same.

Through this awfulness, our friends stayed close to us, sharing their love and support, ever mindful of our pain. I am so grateful for everyone who was there.

Each of us looked into Quinton's room, fully expecting to see him. But he wasn't there, and our last hope that it had been a horrible dream was dashed.

Nobody knew what to say. What do you say in moments like that? Usually when the pain of a loss is fresh, it is best to simply be there. And they were there for us, to comfort us. Kristine immediately went to the master bedroom, lay down, and cried. The ladies went with her, to comfort her. I looked into Quinton's room again, and still he was not there.

The afternoon was a blur. Alex stayed with me, as did Troy Nicholson, but I couldn't tell you for how long. George Linehan came by, and I thanked him for vouching for us with the church. The rest of the day was spent with friends coming and going, including Tony and Joanne Rodriguez; Les, Cheryl, and Stacy Pendleton; Sandrena and Loren Robinson; Quaid and Emi Pauls; and the list of friends and neighbors who circulated through goes on and on.

Kristine spent much of the time in the bedroom, and I was in the family room. Kristine and I were grieving very, very differently, which became more evident when we arrived home. That simple fact would become more evident as the next six weeks unfolded. Kristine cried a lot without speaking much about our loss. On the other hand, while I was pretty lost and didn't know what to do with myself, I wouldn't stop talking about what had happened. My life had a gaping hole where my son had been, and I seemed to be trying to fill that hole with words. I was grateful for the company.

I think I was already sharing the key moments, the divine moments associated with Quinton's journey home at that point. I sensed the apprehension our friends felt in being in our home without Quinton. There was a tendency to be silent in awful situations such as this, but silence was not an option for me and I filled the silence with what had occurred before during and after that fateful moment.

It was either Tuesday or Wednesday night when Mary Beaty, Mike

Carter, and Jenifer Mintle came by. Mary was the wife of my high school football head coach. I last saw her late the prior year when visiting Bob Beaty, not long before he passed away from colon cancer in November. Mike Carter had been the assistant football coach at Evergreen High while we were there and had later become the head football coach. Jenifer was the glue that kept the entire class in loose contact after almost thirty years. It was a touching visit as we filled the silence together with love and memories during such a difficult time.

During the day on Wednesday, June 17, we went to see Quinton at the Evergreen Mortuary. He arrived from Cortez the previous day, and we arranged for a private viewing. I asked Alex and Renee to attend with us. Simply saying "It was tough" doesn't come close to describing what we were feeling and experiencing.

Quinton was just as beautiful as ever. His skin and hair were perfect, only he wasn't breathing. He should have been. *How was it possible? Why?* I wondered. I was still too numb, and the whole scene was surreal. I couldn't spend too much time with him. It was too painful, and I was still running as fast as I could from the feeling of sadness, the feeling of loss. I kissed him, held his hand briefly, and said, "Good-bye, son. I will see you soon."

Cheyanne and Kris spent a lot of time with him, taking pictures, stroking his hair, and holding his perfect hands. Quinton always had the softest, gentlest hands, which we had held when we had gone for walks. Cheyanne held his right hand for so long that warmth returned. All of us kept looking at him in his perfection. We expected him to open his eyes and crack a joke; Cheyanne especially expected that, but it didn't happen.

While Kristine and Cheyanne spent time with what used to be Quinton, I sat on a couch in silence. Alex came over to comfort me, and suddenly, I remembered the dream/vision I'd had on the houseboat. I had forgotten it until that very moment, even about how, after I awoke, I told Kristine and Quinton about the dream and about Quinton's response. It was the way he had said, "It wouldn't happen like that, Dad.

I would just swim away," that came to my mind with force, and I broke down.

I realized that this was yet another message from Quinton then and now. Quinton set us on a new path for our lives. On this new path, we have learned and continue to learn so much, which enables us to better understand what is real. What a mixed bag, what a dichotomy. We now know there is more to our lives, but I can't ruffle my son's hair, hold his hand, play catch with him, go for drives with him, watch *Star Wars* with him, marvel with him at fast cars or big trucks, go for walks with him, or play basketball with him. This is a new normal that can seem joyless at times and wondrous at other times.

On the day before the service, I melted down. My left leg was still swollen and was starting to concern me. While in Farmington, I went to the emergency room to find out what was going on with my leg and discovered that I had a small blood clot below my knee; it didn't require immediate treatment and wouldn't prevent me from flying but would require treatment when I returned home.

I had done all that I could to manage the emotions of everyone who had come to our aid while running hard from my own emotions. At the same time I was working with the team of supporters coordinating our return to Colorado and the service, but I had done little about my leg. Suddenly it all hit me, I had had enough. I needed to see somebody immediately. I called my orthopedic surgeon and left a message early in the morning. By 10:00 a.m., I hadn't heard back, so I decided to call once more.

"This is Ernie Jackson again," I said. "Look, we have been in an accident that took the life of my son. I need someone to look at my leg today." My tone wasn't pleasant on that voice mail.

I was just about to call Leticia Overholt, a doctor in Colorado Springs, to ask if she could see me when I received a call back from my orthopedic doctor's office. I was ready to pop with anger and frustration over the loss of Quinton and poured all of my angst out in dealing with my leg. It seemed easier to be angry than to feel sadness. I apologized for my demeanor as I was told that he would see me, but I only had an hour before he left for another obligation. I thanked the receptionist and told her that I would see her shortly.

He was leaving in an hour, and I lived an hour away. I was out of control as I quickly got dressed and headed for the car. My mom insisted on coming with me; she was worried about me in the mood and state of mind I was in.

"Do you want me to drive?" she asked.

"Nope," I said.

I got down there before the doctor left, but there was a lot of tire squealing along the way.

The doctor came in, and his demeanor changed very quickly as he felt my energy, my angst over the nightmare we were living. Before writing a prescription for Xanax, he checked me over and discovered that my left knee was moving in ways it shouldn't have been moving. He ordered a magnetic resonance imaging scan for the following week (the MRI showed that I had torn my medial collateral ligament in the accident).

Immediately after the exam, he sent me to my family practitioner to have the blood clot in my leg treated. While I was there, they wrote prescriptions for Coumadin pills and Lovenox injections.

Later in the day, after we arrived home, I sat down on a couch downstairs, and somebody put on *Madea Goes to Jail.* Mom intended to give me half of a Xanax, but she gave me three quarters of one. I finally relaxed and passed out five minutes into the movie, receding from reality and the awful pain of knowing that my son was dead.

Chapter Nine

THE SERVICE

Mom wrote, "Going through the preparations for Quinton's homecoming so soon after Barry [her younger brother] and Mom's passing was hard. For them, I knew it was going to happen; with Quinton, I didn't. Saying good-bye to Quinton was the hardest thing I've ever done, and I have had some rough times. While staying with my son, I got to sleep in Quinton's room, and although he was not there in body, I felt close to him. It was comforting for me."

On Wednesday, June 17, Father Jim Baird, dressed casually in Dockers and a polo shirt, came to the house to visit with us before we went to view Quinton. We had never met, but we hit it off immediately as Kristine shared her vision for the service. Kristine was very direct and clear. She wanted it to be a celebration of Quinton's life. She even went so far as to request that everyone attending wear bright colors. We discussed Quinton too. We were together for more than an hour, sharing stories of Quinton, of his spirit and zest for life. Father Jim took it all in with eagerness.

One story we related was about how, given what a gentle spirit Quinton was, he would get teased on occasion by some of his classmates. He would come home to Kristine, not in anger but with questions.

"Mom, why are some of my friends so mean?" he would ask.

When I arrived home, I would invariably say to Quinton, "Son, just knock them down."

But he never did; violence wasn't Quinton's style.

As we relayed that story, Father Jim turned to me with a twinkle in his eye and said, "Sounds like the son was trying to teach the dad." Indeed, of that there is no doubt.

Interestingly, everyone had been a friend to Quinton, whether they were nice to him or not.

Near the end of our visit, Father Jim asked if any of us wanted to speak at the service. I turned to Cheyanne and Kristine; neither volunteered. Up until that moment, I hadn't seriously considered standing up in church and speaking. Normally, I am a very nervous public speaker to the point that I shake in my shoes, but I would speak. I could not sit on the sidelines yet again, not at my son's service. This was my task; I knew it in my soul.

Before the service, Uncle Jim and Aunt Troy flew in from Phoenix. Regina and Jeff flew in from Las Vegas. Kristine's sister, Julie, and our nephews flew in as well—TK and Alexander (a.k.a. Trigger) from Los Angeles. My employer/owner representatives from Schnitzer West flew in from Seattle; Lynda Collie, Kellanne Henry, and Stacy Amrine were all there.

We arrived at the church at 1:30 p.m. on June 19, 2009, and were ushered into a private room. The scene was unreal at the church; it was packed with approximately six hundred of our friends, neighbors, and professional peers. There were so many people! It was an incredible sight for us and for those who knew us. It is a testimony not only Quinton's impact within the community but ours as well within our individual spheres of influence. This point was driven home time and time again as we visited with others long after the service was completed.

It was time to sit down before the service began. We were numb. It was difficult to fathom that this had happened to us. All of us were still hoping to wake up from this nightmare. They told me what Father Jim said was uplifting and that he captured the essence of Quinton's soul. He made clear that we were all there to celebrate Quinton's life with love, but I don't remember any of it. *This cannot be happening* was pretty much what I was thinking.

The next thing I knew, Father Jim asked me to come up. I refused to use my crutches, and I slowly walked up to the podium in measured steps because I didn't want to fall. Afterward, I was told that most of the congregation was surprised to see me stand, walk to the podium, and begin speaking. This was my task, and I would not have been able to live with myself if I hadn't done it.

The church was silent as I stood there at the podium looking out at the congregation. I was kind of floating. While blocking out the physical pain in my body and trying to suppress my emotional pain, I lay Cheyanne's composition book on the podium. When we had still been at the San Juan Regional Medical Center, I had felt the need to write again, much like I had previously. I opened to the page where I had doodled and read my beloved son's eulogy.

> You might think I am a decent guy, but what you should know is my wife, Kristine Carole Cano, is my better half by far. And our son, Quinton Stone Jackson, was the best of both of us.
>
> Quinton was the most loving, kindhearted soul we have ever known. He was always there with a smile and empathy for everybody. Quinton could sense if anyone around him was in pain, and he would be there with concern and a kind word.
>
> As Quinton became older, it became more and more clear that he was more special than we could imagine or understand. His kind and caring soul grew and surpassed our own to the point that, upon quiet reflection, it is evident that he was more than just our son. He was a saint, an angel sent to us by our Father in heaven—on loan as it turned out to be.
>
> Quinton left us with the lessons of how we should live our lives. That lesson is more poignant for some of us than others, but it is an important lesson nevertheless. Be kind and

caring to everyone. Slow down and experience life physically, spiritually, and emotionally. Most of all, be happy while here.

The church was silent during and after the eulogy that I delivered. I was honoring my son, Quinton Stone Jackson. I didn't know until later how it was received.

The service ended quickly. Quinton's ashes and two pictures were near the front of the church between the congregation and the stage where the podium was located. We stood up and walked over to them. George and one of his younger sons, Sean, joined us. We stayed there briefly, not really knowing what came next in the moment or in our lives and numb to what was going on around us. How could this be? Even though we had learned so much about soul contracts, intended experiences, and lessons for our lives, it still seemed wrong for a child to die before his/her parents.

Someone had taken control of the after-service function long before the day of. At that point, the people who wanted to stay for a bite to eat and/or to personally share their condolences with us were directed into a satellite building. Some went inside, but many lined up outside between the church and that building, waiting for us.

We slowly made our way down the aisle to the front doors of the church. We were completely depleted; our emotional and physical weariness lay heavily on our beings. The church foyer was crowded with familiar faces; many were those of my teammates from the class of '83 football team and of some of my friends from that class as well. One of my first clues that my high school teammates were there was when I found myself looking straight ahead into a man's chest. When I looked up, I saw Jonathan Summers; I hadn't seen him in years. Rick Flanagan was there, and I hadn't seen him since we had gone to college together at the University of Wyoming, where we had played football on scholarship. Doug Wills, Bob Pieper, Alex Brister, Coach Carter were there, and the list goes on. I was buoyed and spent the next several minutes visiting with them and thanking all of them for their support.

Meanwhile, Kristine was fading quickly. Mary Gilmer saw this unfolding and got us moving to the reception before Kristine passed out.

There were so many familiar faces, so much love! The love from everyone in attendance and their positive energy lifted our spirits. It was overwhelming, even for me, a man who still struggled to be in touch with his emotions. But there was something else; I felt lifted or buoyed, like I was riding a cushion of air.

We were helped up the stairs and gently guided toward a table set up for us in front of a video screen. We were directed to sit down, which Kristine needed in the worst way. Cheyanne sat next to Kristine. We were given plates of food provided by Troy Tyus, the owner and operator of the now Stagecoach Grill in Evergreen, Colorado. Emi and Quaid Pauls had volunteered to put together a slideshow of Quinton, and they met with Cheyanne upon our return earlier in the week. They found plenty of pictures to work with, including the one of Quinton and I on the sand hill at Lake Powell. The slideshow began, but I couldn't bear to watch. My emotions surged to the surface and threatened to breach the walls. Quickly, I turned away and faced those waiting to express their condolences. It wasn't until many months later that I sat down to watch the slideshow. I cried..

There was a line of people behind us and out the door, a line of people who felt moved to speak to all three of us. I felt a need to speak with them as well. I stood up, turned around, and proceeded to speak with everyone who wished to say a word. We must have been there for two hours, sharing, embracing, and remembering Quinton.

Bill, Jean, and John Lambert were near the front of the line. Bill had been my West Jefferson Junior High Technology Arts teacher, track coach, and assistant football coach. Jean was his wife, and John was his son, whom I had gone to school with. They sat down at the table behind us and visited with my mom after visiting with us.

My coworkers from the Schnitzer West Denver office and their children, whom Quinton had played with once when we had invited them over to our home for a barbeque, came up to pay their respects. The little boys, who were approximately six and eight, were distraught. They had only known Quinton briefly, but it should come as no surprise that he had made a significant impact upon them.

Bryan Dennis and his wife Maggie were there. I went to junior high and high school with Bryan, and he was another I hadn't seen or had contact with since we graduated, but seeing him after twenty-six years, it was like no time had passed. Bryan introduced his wife, who told me that Bryan had told her all about me. I was surprised that I had had an impact on him. He had been my friend, and it had never mattered if I was the starting quarterback or the homecoming king when it came to our friendship, but he clearly stated his belief that our friendship had kept some of the kids from teasing him. Wow! I will always struggle to understand my own impact on the lives of friends, acquaintances, and people I have met over the years.

I was starting to feel woozy, but sitting down did not enter my mind. Mary Gilmer did her best to impress upon me the importance of sitting down, but I brushed her aside while trying not to appear rude. Eventually, Cheryl Pendleton, who had been quietly watching the whole scene, walked up to me with a glass of water and said, "I have been watching you, Ernie. You are pale, and you look like you are going to pass out. Sit down and drink this." I drank it and continued standing to greet those still in line.

So many friends and peers from BOMA Denver and more classmates from high school came: Heidi Dexter, Keri Lee Stickley, Andrea Adamo, and the list goes on.

Eventually, Leticia (Tish) Overholt walked up to me and pointedly told me to sit down. Tish and I had had a special friendship that began while we were both attending West Jefferson Junior High School. She had become a medical doctor and knew that I had a blood clot in my leg. She walked up to me and must have said, "Sit down, now!" I am not sure what it was specifically, but there was no brushing Tish aside; maybe because of the tone in her voice.

Quinton's Messages

I attempted to crack a joke, saying that my doctor told me I had to sit down, but by that point, I knew I needed to get off my feet. While I was still lifted emotionally and spiritually by so much support, I had reached my physical limits. I sat and started grabbing bites of food; I now had two plates of food before me. I continued to greet those near the end of the line of well-wishers.

The reception ended, and we went home to a home that would never be the same.

Todd VanOpdorp had also attended the service and reception. I had known Todd for ten years, and we had worked together several times in our careers. He was one of the hardest-working people that I knew. He sent an e-mail to me on June 20 that described what he had experienced while attending the service and the difference it had made in his life. His message pretty well sums up the service.

Dear Ernie and Kristine,

As I write this, my thoughts continue to be with you and your family. Although I never personally met Quinton, I know he is very special, because he has the both of you for his parents.

As I was driving up to the "Celebration of Quinton's Life," my heart was very heavy and filled with sadness. When I saw the both of you and your family, my heart became even heavier. Then, as the celebration began and I listened to the priest, I realized my heart was heavy because it has an enormous amount of love in it for you and your family. I never understood until yesterday that sadness is the result of so much love; without love, sadness would never exist.

As the celebration continued, my heart felt a little less heavy. Then as I watched Ernie proceed to the front of the church and begin to talk about Quinton, my heart suddenly felt heavy again. As I observed Ernie's incredible strength and listened to his kind, loving, caring, and inspirational words, my heart immediately felt lighter once again. I realized at that time that my life was being touched by Quinton and that, from that day forward, I was going to be a better person because of him.

After the celebration was over, I had the good fortune of sharing a moment with Ernie. As I gave Ernie a hug in an effort to provide comfort, I realized that Ernie was comforting me with his hug and words of wisdom. As I walked away, I realized that Ernie Jackson is truly an incredible father, husband, and person.

As I drove back down the mountain, I reflected on the incredible celebration that had just taken place and realized that my life would be changed forever. As I returned back to the office to complete the day, I did something that I have never done: I left the office at 4:30 p.m. so I could go home and take my youngest son swimming. My son had been asking me to take him swimming for the past week, and I never took the time, always too busy. Because of Quinton and the both of you, I had one of the most enjoyable one-on-one times with my son. For this, I will always be grateful to you.

I only wish there was something I could do for your family in return for how you and Quinton have changed my life forever in such a positive way. Please know that my family and I will always be here for you and your family. By changing my life, you have impacted my entire family's life, touching my heart with so much love and making me strive to be a better father, husband, and person. Thank you so much. Quinton will forever be in my heart!

With Love,
Todd

Chapter Ten

SUMMER OF 2009

Not long after the service, Troy, Cathie, Megan, and Ryan Nicholson came over for an afternoon visit.

As Troy and I sat around our kitchen island, I shared my private doubts that I had been a good father to Quinton. Troy shut me down with such force that I have not ventured down that path again. My perspective was that none of us are perfect and that there is always room for improvement. I mean, come on; let's be honest. But he wasn't having it.

"Ernie, you and Quinton were always together," Troy said. Then he sat silently for a moment and expressed a desire to amend his statement for further clarification to be sure I understood what he was saying. Troy said, "Ernie, I never saw the two of you apart."

He knocked me back on my heels with his very clear and direct statements. *Isn't it odd how many of us focus on the few negative memories or thoughts while completely putting out of our minds the good memories and thoughts that make up the majority?* At that moment, when I started sharing with Troy, I was being honest and reflective, but he wasn't done with me yet. Troy then said, with emotion, "Just in case you still don't understand, when I saw you together with Quinton, I aspired to be as good a father as you." His eyes filled with tears, and mine did as well. I had needed to hear that, not just because of its truth but also because, in that moment, I had forgotten. Often, I forget the good and overemphasize my shortcomings. Being aware of this doesn't make it any easier to overcome.

During the week after the service, our friends purchased and planted a nine-feet-tall blue spruce in our yard to represent and honor Quinton. The height of the tree represented his age. Kristine and I picked a location near the house at the end of our driveway. The tree was purchased from McGarva Landscaping, and Bob Iannaccone dug a hole with his landscape equipment with the help of Troy Nicholson.

After the tree was planted, Kathryn coordinated a tree dedication on the first Sunday after Quinton's service, which was June 21. I was surprised by how many of our closest friends and neighbors were there: John McDonough, Bob Pieper, Troy and Cathie Nicholson, Quaid and Emi Pauls, Tony and Joanne Rodriguez, and the Linehans. All of us were there, along with our nephews TK and Trigger. I was worn out and not feeling well, but I found a spot in the shade. Kathryn conducted a beautiful ceremony, and everyone had the opportunity to leave something around the tree for Quinton.

During the ceremony, we had a visitor. With the poem by John McDonough that we had used on the prayer card fresh on our minds, those in attendance began one by one to notice a hummingbird hovering stationary, directly over Quinton's tree during the entire service. The behavior of the hummingbird was so unusual that most of us knew Quinton was making his presence known.

We have always loved hummingbirds, but their behavior that summer was extraordinary. Often, one would hover near us. One morning, Cheyanne heard something hit one of our family room windows. When she went outside, she found a hummingbird lying on the deck. Cheyanne picked it up and put it on the rail. I came outside not long afterward, picked up the unconscious hummingbird, and sat in a chair, holding it in my hand, gently stroking it. I sat there for at least ten minutes while holding the hummingbird, wondering why the hummingbird had been trying to get into our home. They have flown all around our home for years, but that was the first time one of them had actually flown into a window. Eventually, the bird began to stir, and it finally took off out of my hand and settled into a nearby tree, where it stayed for some time.

Quinton's Messages

One afternoon, Kristine came out the front door and stood on the landing as one of our friends was leaving; all of a sudden, there was a hummingbird hovering directly in front of her face only a foot away. The hummingbird hovered in front of Kristine for several minutes before flying away.

For some, it may be easier to try and explain away occurrences such as these in an effort make our reality more understandable or less unknown. In doing so, they use words like coincidence or unusual or odd to explain it all away and make themselves feel more in control or at least provide themselves with the illusion that we know what is going on in our world. That summer we learned a different truth; these coincidences and odd or unusual occurrences are truly where the magic is! These events speak to the simple fact that, there is more to our world than meets the eye.

As I mentioned, George and Mary Linehan attended the dedication with their children, and they saw the hummingbird and heard the discussion. Not long afterward, George stopped by with a fall edition of *St. Anthony Messenger*[1], and he directed me to read an article by Marion Amberg on signs from loved ones. For some reason, I was surprised this information was in a religious magazine.

The entire article discussed experiences such as ours, but one stood out. A woman in her thirties lost her sister to cancer. After her sister's funeral, the family went to a lake cabin for solitude and to grieve for their loss. While they were there, a wild bird landed on the shoulder of the surviving sister's husband and then flew over and perched on the porch swing that her deceased sister had loved to sit in. Suddenly and strangely, the bird made a noise that sounded like the deceased sister's laughter! My friends, there is so much more to our existence and to our lives.

----

1 Amberg, Marion. 2009. "Surrounded by Saints." St. Anthony Messenger. November. www.americancatholic.org/messenger/Nov2009/feature3.asp.

Meals were coming daily, and most were personally delivered. We were usually successful at being there when the meals arrived. Typically, our friends delivering the meals had a higher priority, that being to spend some time with us.

At this point, I began to drive Kristine crazy by always talking about the accident. I mentioned earlier that grieving differently is normal and to be expected. We learned this firsthand and have subsequently read this simple fact in print on numerous occasions. Kristine grieved as one might expect; she was very emotional and expressive of the pain associated with Quinton's transition. Me, not so much . . . my sadness and tears still come in waves and usually in private. I do find it interesting that I am sadder now, in 2011, than in the previous two years. My sense of the loss of my son, my buddy, weighs heavily on my mind as our lives continue to change.

Invariably, when each individual or family came, I shared the details of what happened to us. This sharing was the beginning of putting it together for myself, and as I did so, the bigger picture began to emerge. What happened to us speaks of so much more. As it came together in my mind, I had to share, and I shared from a sense of amazement as I realized what I was saying. I would share, and people would cry as they understood the implications of our experiences. All of a sudden, I was imparting experiences that I had very little, if any, previous conscious knowledge of. I was discussing spirituality and metaphysics, and I shared without fear, because it was what had happened to us; it was our experience. While I cannot explain why there is so much *apparent* misery in the world, why there is disease and warfare, I can discuss with authority what happened to us, no matter how unbelievable some may find it. I shared openly and honestly, without fear of what anybody would think, and I continue to.

Something very interesting happened along the way. As I shared information and thoughts outside the realm of typical conversation, the people I shared with began to share similar happenings of their own contact with transitioned loved ones. It was like they hadn't shared before because of a fear that what they had experienced would not be accepted by our society, their friends, and their neighbors. They didn't want to be thought of in a negative way, as loony. But after hearing our experiences, they became comfortable and shared with us what they never would have shared with us before. We continue to be amazed by the commonality of our experiences.

This went on all through the rest of June and July. I was always sharing—at the house, at neighborhood gatherings, even at the store. Some of our other neighbors, Charles and Jenny Holzworth, were having cookouts that many of the neighbors attended every Thursday evening. I shared the message with people there. One afternoon, Jennifer Baltus brought a meal for us. I had worked with Jennifer while at ING Clarion Realty Services. I had always admired and looked up to Jennifer, but I did not know if she was ready to hear what I had to say. Now understanding why I was on the planet at this time, I knew I had to share, even if the person in front of me might not be receptive. I launched in, while prefacing with my concern that she might not be receptive to what I had to say. Quickly, it became clear that I did not really know Jennifer as well as I had thought. She was all in; she directed me to speak with two other individuals who had had similar experiences.

In July of 2009, I tried to go back to work; I wasn't sure why at the time. Budget season was coming up, which is an extremely busy time of the year for those of us in the field of property management, and I thought I could lend a hand. I had the impression that I could come back in a different capacity. My position with Schnitzer West dictated that I control essentially every facet of the commercial asset operation from a local perspective, while my personality lends itself to me being more of a leader by example and a provider of positive energy. I tried to come back, not as the leader but only help the existing team while continuing to find my bearings in a new reality.

My return was not what I had expected, and I soon realized that I had come back to share our experiences, which were fast becoming a message. My first day back was very emotional. I showed up in a melancholy mood, and the staff and I did a lot of reminiscing. We talked about Quinton and their visit to our home in Conifer, and I shared the details of what had opened our eyes to a larger reality.

After a short period of time, I tried to get back into the normal work routine, but it wasn't the same. First, I didn't have any positive energy to share with the staff, and unfortunately, they were unable to generate enough to buoy me. Second, all of the things I had thought were important before—reports, deadlines, and procedures—no longer seemed even remotely important. Lastly, I spent an inordinate amount of time either on the phone or meeting with tenants in person to share the message. I hadn't realized the strength of the bonds that I had formed in a short year on the properties in Cherry Creek, Colorado.

There was a lot going on upon my return. As I watched my performance and the attitudes in the office from a higher perspective of observation, I knew within a couple of weeks that I had to leave. The company mentioned the possibility of me taking short-term disability, and upon the realization that I wasn't ready to come back, I accepted.

Before I left Schnitzer West on disability, Melissa Chaffin called my office. Melissa was one of those whom Jennifer Baltus had mentioned to me. I pointedly told her that I had been told to speak with her. She had the same energy and eagerness to meet with me as I had to meet with her. We scheduled a lunch for the week of July 19. Not knowing what to expect, Kristine and I met with Melissa at a Whole Foods deli for a late lunch. After introductions and buying lunch, we sat down.

Melissa quickly shared that her father transitioned earlier in the year. She had been there when he had transitioned, and she confided in us that she had seen the most amazing thing: she had seen his spirit leave his body. She had our attention; we were all ears. She went on to say that, later in the week of his transition, her family ended up together at her father's home in an impromptu informal celebration of his life. During their visit, Melissa explained, "As I sat in my father's chair, I soon realized that he was within me, using my eyes to take in the gathering with pleasure." This is yet another example of what happens when we share our experiences. In sharing, we often are blessed to hear the amazing experiences of others.

Before we could even ask a question, Melissa changed subjects by informing us that she had attended Quinton's service. She indicated that, while she was there, Quinton had come to her and said, "I am so happy you are here." Our mouths dropped open, and tears filled our eyes. The agreed-upon interpretation was that Quinton was pleased that Melissa was there, because she was able to hear him. He added, as she could clearly understand, that he was happy and enjoying himself, that he was fine. Melissa had the impression that he was playing and laughing while imparting his message. Then he had said something that she didn't really understand. Quinton said, "Let my father know that my passing was intended to change his life." Both mine and Kristine's jaws hit the table. We had absolutely no clue what Melissa had wanted to share with us, and we were completely unprepared for another message from Quinton. While we expressed gratitude to Melissa for sharing, we tried to digest what we had just heard.

This was our second indirect message from Quinton, and it kept us on the path. It made sure our eyes were still open.

Chapter Eleven

QUINTON'S VISITS

Up to that point, we weren't aware of receiving any direct messages, but we were still filled with awe and wonder. I hadn't yet understood the significance of the sensation of having my hand held in Farmington while lying in bed not long after we had first arrived there. The next visitations would be indisputable, even for me.

I have always been dead set against any form of body piercings and tattoos, because I believed both would be frowned upon within the professional circles I traveled in, but after Quinton was called home, I knew I would wear his earring in my left ear. Before the month of June ended, Cheyanne and I drove down to a local mall. Cheyanne was adding an earring, and I was getting my ear pierced. I wore the temporary stud for two weeks, per instructions, and then put in one of Quinton's earrings. I had intended on wearing the black u-shaped earring that he was wearing when he was called home, but somehow I managed to misplace it. Now I wear his polished steel u-shaped earring instead.

Every night, I diligently cleaned his earring in my left ear with the recommended solution to avoid infection. One night in August, I took a shower in the kids' bathroom. It was a Wednesday before August 23. When I finished, I dried myself off, put on my pajamas, and opened the door. Steam fogged the mirror, but it started to dissipate immediately upon my opening the door. As the mirror cleared, I cleaned Quinton's earring in my ear. His bedroom was directly across the hallway from the bathroom, so I could see the reflection of his room in the mirror. As I cleaned my ear and the earring, I saw a silhouette walk across Quinton's room from west to east. I stopped what I was doing immediately, turned around, and walked into Quinton's room, expecting to find Kristine, Cheyanne, or TK in the room. Nobody was there. I stood in Quinton's doorway, staring in amazement.

The rest of the family sat in the family room and asked me what I was doing. I told them that I saw Quinton. I saw him, his silhouette. He seemed a little taller, but I knew it was him. I was beside myself with awe and wonder as Kristine wisecracked, "What took you so long?" I laughed, but didn't know exactly how to take her comment, because she had indicated that she hadn't seen him yet. Not wanting to cause her any pain, I didn't pursue it with her.

On the morning of September 16, a little later in the summer, I arose first, which has always been typical for me. I climbed out of bed and shuffled down the hallway at about six fifteen in the morning. As I walked past Quinton's bedroom, he called my name—just one word, "Dad," and that one word was all I needed to know it was him. It was his voice. I, Mr. Oblivious, was having my own moments of extrasensory perception. It caught me off guard, and I wasn't sure what to do. I was so excited as I paused and then continued on toward the kitchen. I wish I had stopped and replied, "Hey Quinton, how are you?" as I have on so many other occasions.

The visit from Quinton that made the most impact on me came in the form of a dream/vision on October 20, 2009. My alarm went off at 5:00 a.m., because I had intended to drive down the hill to 24 Hour Fitness for a workout, but I decided I needed more sleep instead. Within minutes of turning the alarm off, I was in a deep sleep again, and Quinton came. In this crystal clear vision, I was on the east side of our home under the deck that overlooked where our sanctuary was located. The sanctuary was a twenty-by-thirty-foot area of grass that we had installed years before on leveled ground. We used large rocks from the yard as a wall to hold the dirt in place, planted aspen trees around the perimeter of the area, and added sod as the finishing touch. In fact, at the end of the day when we were installing the aspen trees in June of 2003, we had received news that Kristine's dad, Edgar Cano, had suffered a massive heart attack. Ed transitioned on June 8. It was in that sanctuary that we placed a memorial for Ed.

In the vision, I stood on the grass. The shadows from the deck rails were at my feet. Those shadows included the shadow of a hooded figure. I immediately knew it was Quinton standing on the deck above me. At that point, I hadn't seen Quinton's face since the accident, and I didn't expect to see his face, but that didn't stop me from looking up and turning around in an attempt to see him. I fully expected Quinton to dissolve before my eyes, but he didn't. His hair was short, as if Kristine or TK had just given him a buzz cut. I saw his face as he pulled his hood off his head; that was how clear the vision was. But there was more: I saw the expressions on his face. He was surprised that I could see him, and he was eager for something. Still asleep and within the vision, I briefly wondered what he was eager for as I choked on his name.

"Quinton! Quinton," I called excitedly as I began the ascent back to consciousness. He saw me waking up and quickly threw off his robe and jumped off the deck toward me. Because I was waking up so quickly, I don't know specifically if I caught him in my arms—I had my arms out, prepared to do so—or if he jumped into me. As I opened my eyes, I was overcome with the most amazing sense of peace, and I believe it was the latter. Quinton had just let me know that he was with me always! That experience has left me feeling the most exquisite sense of peace I have ever felt.

I shared these visits from Quinton often, but I tried not to share too frequently within earshot of Kristine, because she hadn't had as intense of experiences as I had had up to that point. That changed early in 2010, when Kristine had her first visitation. Some people have written that if you are filled with too much negative energy, your transitioned loved ones may have a difficult time making contact. There is another school of thought that suggests that some may not see their transitioned loved ones, because they are always with them. We believe Kristine to have been in the latter group.

Kristine commented that she often dreamed of Quinton and felt as if he was hiding from her. In those dreams, Quinton laughed and played while calling out to Kristine. Finally, one night he was there. Kristine had gone to sleep, and one of her earrings was hurting her. While she was sleeping Quinton came to her in a vision. In her vision he had bloodshot eyes, as if he was in pain because she was in pain and then he spoke, "You don't have to hurt anymore, Mom. It will be okay." When she awoke in the morning, she saw the earring that had been hurting her had mysteriously been removed from her ear and placed neatly on her pillow. Since then, Kristine has had visits while awake. How many of us have seen movement out of the corner of our eye only to turn toward the movement and see nothing?

Mary Gilmer shares, "I was riding my bike near the top of Armadillo Trail listening to a Christian radio station. The pastor was speaking about how to answer parents who had a child die. 'Why did my child die?' The pastor said he did not understand either, and perhaps we would all have that knowledge when we got to heaven like the Bible promises. He did try to answer the parents' question with the answer of:

'Perhaps the children who die so young are being spared from the pain and sufferings of living their entire lives in our world.' I thought I needed to call Kristine right away, maybe that answer would be of comfort to her. When I was thinking of calling her, a hummingbird circled above me and then hovered directly in front of my face while I was riding my bike. I felt it was the spirit of Quinton. I called Kristine, and she then told me other stories of hummingbirds visiting her and the family."

And the beat goes on, as Quinton continues to send messages or signs of his presence.

The Psychic

I had never seriously considered spending time with a psychic prior to Quinton going home, and I don't know why exactly. As I sit here and reflect, I no longer remember my mind-set on the topic, but I do know that I had never intended to see a psychic. I expect I was afraid of what I would discover or afraid that I would learn just how small my view of reality was.

When Kristine was still working at Heaney Family Chiropractic, Regina Quarles provided massages for Maggy Heaney's clients. Regina continues to be a friend, and she had been providing us with regular massages since the accident. After one of her sessions, we discussed possibly sitting for a reading, and she directed us to a local psychic. I made an appointment with Leianne Wilson.

The appointed day came, and I went to Leianne's home office and rang the doorbell. When she opened the door, we both beamed at each other and said hi. She ushered me in. While we made small talk, I was trying to be positive to cover my apprehension. One of Leianne's gifts is her positive energy, which she gives freely to all her clients, and slowly the apprehension that I felt dissolved after I followed her up her stairs to the studio, and we began the reading.

As instructed, I brought a list of questions. Looking at the list of questions now, I realize which questions were completely irrelevant and which were important. Some of them were: Where will I live in the future? Which state? What career should I pursue? Am I a good person or a bad person? What are my strengths and weaknesses from a character perspective? When will I die? I haven't read these questions since I wrote them in July of 2009. It is clear that I was just beginning to understand that I didn't know who I was and was beginning a journey to better understand myself on all levels. The more relevant questions pertained to Quinton, of course. The answers to those questions would also propel me to an unknown path, leading to an unknown destination; it is this path that I now find myself on. Those questions included the following: Is Quinton happy? What does Quinton do while in heaven? When will I see him again? Did Quinton love me?

From a certain perspective, the reading began when I called to make the appointment when we felt each other's energy. Yeah, I know; in today's day and age, some might not understand what I mean and think I am off my rocker. I have just recently begun to understand interactions with others in these metaphysical terms myself. It is safe to say that all of us have had the experience of hitting it off with someone or being drawn inexplicably to someone to someone in some way; this is what I mean when I say we felt each other's energy. I think many of us mistake this feeling with sexual attraction, but more often than not, it isn't that. When I showed up for the reading, that feeling, that continuing to feel and become acquainted with each other's energy resumed.

The actual reading began with a deck of cards. Leianne had me break the cards into three relatively equal stacks, and she never looked at them again. The next thing I knew, Leanne had tapped into the essence of Quinton; her voice didn't change or anything like that, but Quinton was communicating through her.

Quinton shared that he and Cheyanne had helped each other grow in previous lives; they were soul buddies. He asked to converse as an adult, because that was his nature, and he wanted me to grasp that his is a special soul that can fracture into parts, thereby allowing him to visit with different individuals at the same time. Quinton indicated that he is most typically on my right shoulder, but eventually, I would hear him in my left ear, which is where his earring is. He added that Cheyanne would gain the most from his planned departure. For those of you unfamiliar with this concept, it relates to our soul contracts, specifically his soul contract, which clearly included dying at a young age.

Quinton continued by saying that his transition was a catalyst for the new path I found myself on, but that I had been on the path already. He said that he had "signed up" for our family because he liked the energy and knew what his impact would be.

At that point in the reading, Quinton became animated. He wanted us to know that the accident hadn't hurt. He drove the point home by stating that he had been out of his body for a full three minutes before the accident had occurred. Quinton remembered looking at his hand and "It was like it didn't work right." I later corroborated this with Cheyanne and Nellie; they both distinctly remembered him looking at his hand before he stepped outside the Suburban for the last time.

Quinton indicated that I was about to get steeped in the metaphysical and that he was proud of me. He next said that most people take three to five years to accept the transition of a loved one, but I had begun to accept his transition in the second or third week as I ventured into metaphysics with the realization that he was there in the form of energy, more commonly known as spirit. Quinton told me that he saw me speaking in schools., which would be confirmed in eight months with a feeling like a light bulb coming on. He said he would be with us forever, but that part of him played while another part of him stayed with Cheyanne to support her as our backbone supports our bodies. He said that he walked around us all the time; he purposefully moved around so we would notice him. He was always trying to get our attention and wanted us to know that he was around.

Well, Quinton, I thought, *it's working, because I notice you from time to time. Thank you, son!*

When the reading took place, Quinton indicated that he would be frustrated, because when I asked him "How are you doing?" I couldn't hear his responses. He indicated that I would begin to sense/hear him in my left ear; after eight to nine months, I would be able to speak to him.

I am still waiting, Quinton. I know you are trying to get my attention as I try to quiet my mind. Soon, we will be talking. At the same time son, I do have to acknowledge the ringing I hear in my left ear from time to time!!

When the reading started, Leianne very pointedly told me not to ask about the future as the future contains several paths with different outcomes. But I had to ask if I would die in 2010. I explained that I had been fixated with the year 2010 for at least ten years and that I was currently thinking that I would go to be with Quinton in that year. Leianne laughed as she said, "No. 2010 will be your year of awakening not death." She indicated that I was taking my prerequisite courses at the time and that I would experience another shift of awareness in 2010, which came to pass.

The Presentation (July 2009)

As the summer of 2009 continued, even though I was pinched off from my emotions, I could feel the sadness coming. At times, I was down and feeling deflated. I continued to share, but I noticed that it was becoming difficult to do so at times. Consequently, I had a desire to share with a larger group before the sadness enveloped me.

While I was attending the annual BOMA Denver golf tournament, I found it difficult to share Quinton's messages. I could not bear the thought of sharing repetitively with so many people individually in one afternoon. The feeling of love coming from my friends and professional peers was overwhelming, and everybody was happy to see me, but I didn't share much. When the tournament ended, there was a meal, awards were given out, and a raffle was held. I ate and left alone, still walking with a slight limp from the accident. For some reason, I always tried to creep out of functions I attended alone and unnoticed, and that occasion was no different.

During that day though, I mentioned to Sheri Pe'a, a friend and fellow BOMA member, that I had a desire to share in front of a larger audience. Within two weeks, I found myself doing so. Sheri worked with fellow BOMA members Karen Pump, Marcia Pryor, and Paul Miller to find a location, date, and time. My longtime friend, Carol Guimarin, owner of High Country Chemical, volunteered her conference room. The team assembled around me was much smarter than I was, and someone within the group suggested that the session be videotaped. Jim Havey was called and volunteered without reservation. It was set.

Meanwhile, Kristine was completely fed up with me. One day, she verbally attacked me.

"You just enjoy telling the story," she said. "Do you even know your son has died?"

How could you say such a thing to me? I thought. I didn't have it in me to be angry. It was a tough time for us; we continued to grieve quite differently, but I knew being angry with or lashing out at my wife would make an already very difficult situation considerably worse. I didn't respond. I could not have said anything kind or productive at that moment. I walked away and left her to her opinion.

Kristine knew nothing of the presentation scheduled for 3:00 p.m. on July 29.

I thought about preparing a script, but I knew that wouldn't work. I was a little nervous speaking in front of a group. After impacting so many people with the message individually, I wasn't sure I would have the same impact on a group, but I needed to do it. I had prepared an outline, but didn't use it. I had also typed the eulogy and made copies for distribution, along with an eight-by-ten collage put together by Mary Gilmer that included the obituary as it had appeared in the *Canyon Courier/High Timber Times*, the prayer card with John McDonough's poem, and the memorial card. I told Cathie Nicholson about the presentation, and she expressed a desire to attend.

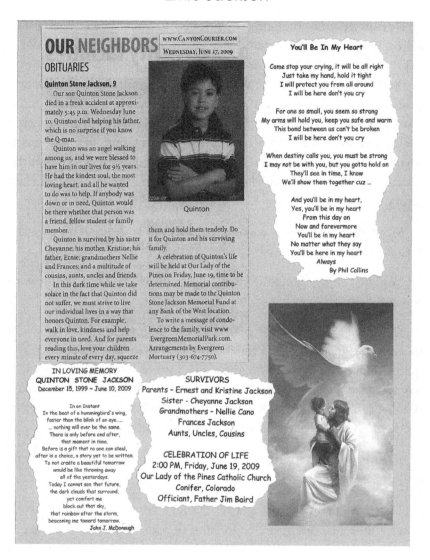

Quinton's collage—done by Mary Gilmer

On the day of the presentation, I casually asked Kristine, "Hey honey, I am sharing our recent experiences in front of my friends and peers at the High Country Chemical office, would you like to attend?" Much to my surprise she accepted. After her verbal attack, I didn't expect she would accept and had extended an invitation just to be polite.

Quinton's Messages

When we arrived, I was tired and unsure how to begin the presentation, but at the same time, I was serene in the knowledge that I was doing what I was supposed to be doing. We arrived early and had plenty of time to hand out the prepared material and relax. After sitting down near the front, we visited with our friends. I shared with someone who was also early that I thought I would start with the accident, which was the first real eye-opener, and then go from there. That person told me that would be a good approach, because many still didn't know specifically what had happened.

So that was where I started. For thirty-two minutes, I spoke, sharing what had happened to us. After describing the accident, I read the obituary and eulogy and provided narrative regarding what was divinely channeled through me. Then I finished with a summary that drove home Quinton's messages in one concise ending.

I never looked at my watch, nor did I have any clue that I had been up there at the podium for thirty-two minutes. I spoke from the heart and was buoyed by the emotions of those in attendance. A connection was made; the emotions I saw in the crowd were the same emotions I had witnessed when sharing Quinton's messages with individuals. At one point, Esperanza Malia, who was seated directly to my right, started crying. I turned to her very briefly, smiled, and gently told her not to cry. On the surface, what had happened to us was the greatest tragedy to befall any parent, but on the other hand, the way it had happened was the most amazing gift. Everything that had happened before the accident, during the accident, and in the messages afterward all pointed in one direction: to a divine source, to the One, the Divine, God, Christ, or whatever name you feel most comfortable with. All of this left us knowing that we are part of something larger than our individual selves.

At the very end of the presentation, I summarized by reviewing and restating the messages we had learned from Quinton. The first is that we must live life to the fullest. If we are parents, we need to spend time with our kids; if they want to do something with us, we should do it. The other message, the broader message, is that there is a higher power right here and right now. I think Quinton is here right now. Before the accident, I often wondered why I was here. Not anymore. I knew why I was here; it was in part to share these messages and Quinton's love, his energy!

Once I had finished, everybody came to Kristine and me one by one to share their thoughts and condolences, to validate our thoughts, to comment on the presentation, and to thank us for having the courage to share our experiences.

After I explained that I had no choice in the sharing, because I felt I had survived the accident to share, we discussed what to do with the video. It was too large for YouTube, so Joe Havey and his assistant put it on Vimeo. The presentation is on the Internet today (visit www.vimeo.com/7314888 or simply go to Vimeo.com and search "Ernie Jackson Presentation"). The link is on my Facebook page, and I continue to share hardcopy DVDs with those who wish to have one; this is a message that must be shared, especially in the materialistic reality we live in today in the western world. When I do provide these DVDs, I give them away at no charge.

Kristine and I left High Country Chemical after most of the group had gone. We gathered up the extra handouts and walked to our vehicle. One the way home, Kristine turned to me and said, "This isn't a story; it is a message." Somehow, she had been able to see through the eyes of those in attendance on that day. In doing so, she was able to see the message that I had been trying to impart all along.

Building Owners and Managers Association Garden Party (August 5, 2009)

Kristine and I attended the annual BOMA Denver Garden Party at the Botanic Gardens. We were both still healing physically, so we quickly found a table and sat down after going through the line to get plates of food. We sat down and were almost immediately joined by friends who wanted to know how we were getting along and to comment on Quinton's messages. It is kind of strange; though I know I remain here in this physical realm to share the message, at times I get tired of hearing my own voice and worry that I am preaching. This event was no different. I had intended to visit quietly and not get on my soapbox. As usual, I didn't.

A good friend was sharing dreams of her first love, who had transitioned years before, and relating how those dreams occurred at the perfect times, usually when she needed support or advice. It was yet another example of people sharing their experiences, which are just as rich as ours. As we had learned personally and through reading, our loved ones are able to communicate with us much more easily while we are asleep, when our minds are not racing with superfluous thoughts. I loved these conversations; all of a sudden, I was in the moment, sharing and receiving the larger picture of our existence.

Before we left, two individuals came up to us separately to share that they had been in attendance at our presentation. One of them said, "During the presentation, I saw your aura; it was green with a yellowish tint. I saw Kristine's aura too, and it was the same but with one key difference; Kristine's aura had a white band at the top." They explained to us that a green aura represented growth and balance and, most of all, something that leads to change. A yellow-green aura represented creativity of heart and communicability. We were also told that our auras are never white; that color represented a higher entity. We quickly concluded that it was Quinton! This was the first time either of us had heard of auras, their colors, and what the colors meant.

The Benches

Two benches were made in Quinton's honor, and two separate bench dedications took place. The first bench was built during the months of July and August with a goal of completing it before the neighborhood kids, and Quinton's friends, went back to school for the fall session in 2009. Once again, our friends Kathryn and Colin Price spearheaded the effort that involved many of our friends and neighbors at the top of Shadow Mountain Road, right after it turns into Black Mountain Road.

Our friends and neighbors decided to install the bench in our neighborhood, specifically at the bus stop used by Quinton and his friends. The stop was located at the corner of Griffin Drive and Black Mountain Road and was on private property. The property owner's name is Dan Bartlett. He lived in his home with his daughter, Angela, but his wife had passed away years before when his daughter was still young. Somebody in the community had approached Dan and asked if the bench could be located on the corner of his lot, and he had readily agreed.

With that settled, Colin designed the bench. Kathryn and Colin owned an iron works business, so he had the material and the know-how to design a mostly steel bench. They did something that I will be forever grateful for; they insisted on my involvement. After some phone tag, I met Colin in his home workshop and took part in welding the legs of the bench to the base plates, which would be bolted onto a concrete pad. We arc welded, which is welding done with an electric current. I would love to say that I hadn't done that since my junior high school technology arts class with Mr. Lambert, but that isn't the case. In ninth grade at the tender age of fifteen, I already knew I would be attempting to get a college scholarship playing football, and I refused to participate in the arc welding portion of the course, because I was worried that I might accidently be blinded. Funny that I was arc welding my son's bench twenty-nine years later without a care for my vision. I suspect Colin was being kind when he repeatedly praised the welding I was doing. I have to admit, it wasn't half bad, but I don't know if he was being sincere when he told me that he would gladly hire me to be a part of his crew!

On the other hand, maybe Quinton was helping me yet again. The annual Building Owners and Managers Association golf tournament put on by the Denver chapter is a great case in point given that I golf even worse than I fish. Typically, I am lucky if I hit the ball, but during the eighteen rounds of golf I played on July 16, I spent the entire time with my mouth hanging open. I was completely amazed by how many good shots I made. The group of ladies I was golfing with let me know that they thought I was sandbagging when I said I golfed poorly. That round of golf and the welding were both clear indications that Quinton was helping me, but the best was yet to come.

Quinton's Messages

The lumber for the seat and the backrest of the bench were donated and prepared by Charles and Jenny Holzworth. The finishing touch would be a forged Q embedded in the front of the backrest. Colin invited me to his shop on Highway 285 to forge the Q. I didn't have a clue what I was doing, so Colin gave me a quick tutorial and started one for me. I finished the rest, and that was the forged Q we screwed into the bench at the dedication ceremony.

Bob and Sue Iannaccone, our neighbors who own a landscaping/snow removal company, donated the concrete and labor for the pad. After the concrete had been poured, we stopped by while it was setting, and Kristine wrote "Rest in Peace: Quinton Stone Jackson" in the concrete.

On August 22, the community had a block party in the cul-de-sac on Griffin Drive. There were at least forty friends and neighbors there, including children. It was potluck, and everyone brought side dishes and their beverages of choice; Greg Jones brought the meat and grill.

Before we sat down to eat, all of us walked up to the top of Griffin drive for the bench dedication. It was emotional for all of us. Kristine and I screwed the forged Q into the location that had been routed out as pictures were taken. Afterward, Kristine, Cheyanne, TK, and I sat on the bench for pictures, and then the neighborhood kids sat on the bench for pictures. In an attempt to combat the feeling of sadness, I tried cracking a joke: "Cheyanne, you will be responsible for sanding and refinishing the bench every couple of years." She looked at me with tears in her eyes, and said, "This isn't the time for jokes." There's nothing like being "told" by your daughter.

Then we went back down to the cul-de-sac for good food and fellowship with our friends and neighbors.

My August 23 journal entry reads:

> You know, Quinton, the more I share, the more I receive in return. And what I receive in return is rich and full of

love and knowledge. Is this the way of the universe, the way of living a full life? I think so. Quinton, you are everywhere. You were here yesterday at the block party at the dedication of your bench, playing with all the kids into the night. Everyone was so happy—parents and children alike. It was beautiful! A hot day turned into a wonderful evening as the stars came out and a lightning storm encroached from the west. You were there, and it is comforting to know this!

As I recall that night now, our eyes were drawn to the forest after the sun went down, and we saw something in the trees. We could not take our eyes off it. My rational mind thought that maybe it was a billowing sheet or a piece of plastic about thirty feet off the ground, while Kristine saw a single red balloon, Quinton's favorite color. We were not aware of when it left, but it was gone in the morning. Sue Iannaccone commented privately to Kristine afterward that it was Quinton letting us know that he was there. The fact that both of us saw two entirely different things isn't so odd when much later we learned that the medicine man that had appeared to Chris and Layla Vodrich looked different to them as well; to Chris the medicine man was in full ceremonial attire while to Layla he was dressed in jeans and a shirt. I have no logical explanation other than, it seems our individual knowledge base directly impacts our perception of the paranormal.

The second bench dedication took place on a cold spring Friday: April 16, 2010. Quinton's Cub Scout troop built the bench with the help of Kristine's friends, Tony and Cassie Clem, who donated material from their deck-building company, Add a Deck. Once again, Katherine and Colin Price donated two metal Qs. I tried to help with the Qs, but Colin cut them out of slab steel, and that was beyond anything I could do even with Quinton's help.

I had arthroscopic and microfracture surgery on my left knee on April 9, 2010, and therefore was on crutches. I took the impact from the airborne car on my left side on June 10. Aside from the road rash, a blood clot, and a small broken bone in my left foot, I also tore my medial collateral ligament. The obvious assumption would be that the surgery was related to the accident; the answer is it was not directly. I have spent much of the time since the accident in the gym channeling my emotions into weightlifting. I eventually ended up squatting and doing heavy leg extensions, which are both exercises that I knew I shouldn't be doing. Well, between the lifting and taking a fall on the football field in March while playing catch, I dislodged a centimeter-long piece of cartilage. Subsequently, I was on crutches at the bench dedication that took place on April 16.

This event was overwhelming. I almost broke down as I looked at Quinton's troop and thought, *Where is Quinton? He should be with them.*

Quinton's troop consisted of approximately twelve boys, and all were in uniform. They lined up as they performed the flag ceremony that is always performed at cub scout meetings. It seemed that fifty people were there, maybe more, and I was surprised by how many people were there. I stood as far back as I could from the crowd as I tried to take it all in and keep from crying.

The dedication took place at Quinton's elementary school, Marshdale. The principle and teachers were there, along with many students and parents. Afterward, some felt moved to share with us about their Quinton sightings. At the time, I was amazed that he was still visiting, and now I wonder why I was so surprised. I think I need to keep reading the words written in this book so I don't lose sight of what is real, you know, the big picture.

The parents of one of Quinton's classmates shared their son's dream of Quinton not long after he was called home. Their son, Jackson, said that Quinton, another friend, and he were outside playing in his dream. There was a staircase, and Quinton was at the top. Quinton guided them up one at a time, telling each of them to be careful. When they arrived at the top, they spent some time together, and Quinton told them that he was okay and everything would be all right. What an amazing message!

Mrs. Capretta, Quinton's second-grade teacher, had an astounding visit from Quinton just a couple of weeks before the dedication of the second bench. Once, while Quinton was in second grade, Mrs. Capretta's nephew had substituted for her; he and Quinton had hit it off. Two weeks before the bench dedication, Mrs. Capretta had been sitting at her desk after a long day, staring at a picture of her nephew that sits on her desk. As she sat at her desk, she wondered why she was mesmerized by her nephew's picture. Then she suddenly realized that she wasn't staring at her nephew at all—she was looking into Quinton's smiling face within the picture frame. Another wow; I continue to be amazed. He is still here with us and others, letting us know he is okay and reminding us of what most of us have forgotten. There is more to our reality than we realize, and the circumstances we find ourselves in are temporary.

Winter Visit with the Psychic (March 4, 2010)

On March 4, 2010 I went back to the psychic, Leianne Wilson, with a different set of questions. The answers to some of those questions linked directly to some of the reading I had been doing since Quinton's transition in my effort to learn more about the suddenly significantly larger reality I suddenly found myself a part of.

"Quinton, what have you been doing?" Quinton said he had been playing and mentioned that he liked to spook the dog. While having fun, he said, he kept watch over us, which was consistent with the July message. He added again that he was more comfortable speaking from his older soul perspective as opposed to the child knew. Quinton finished answering that question by saying he had been taking classes and was interested in participating in more. That comment struck a chord with me, because much of my reading indicated that that is indeed what we do when we leave the physical realm before we return. This concept was first introduced to me in the *Mathew* books by Susan Ward.

"Quinton, are you preparing to come back?" Quinton quickly responded no. He indicated that he was in the best place to serve for the next ten to fifteen years and that he needed a break. Based upon our knowledge that Quinton is an advanced soul, his answers came as no surprise. Clearly, Quinton was part of our lives to teach us.

"Quinton, how many lifetimes have you lived?" Quinton's response was that he had lived fifteen full lifetimes and fifteen lifetimes in which he had shared lives via piggybacking. I was a little surprised at this response, given I had read *Many Lives, Many Masters* by Brian Weiss, which shared his experience with a patient who had lived eighty-six lives. I had expected Quinton to have lived more, but the comment about shared lifetimes struck a chord because I had also read about piggybacking. Essentially, a soul piggybacks when it joins another physical being (with their own soul), to have experiences that soul hasn't had before. It is important to note that, when this happens, the visiting soul does not interfere and is only there to partake in the experience. When I shared this with Leianne afterward, she was noticeably relieved; she wasn't entirely familiar with the concept that Quinton spoke of and was concerned that she shared it inaccurately.

"Quinton, what age are you most comfortable being?" I had to ask that question, because Quinton had commented in both readings that he wished to speak from an older perspective. Quinton replied that he was most comfortable speaking between the ages of twenty-six and forty-five years old. He indicated that, when he was being playful, he did so at the age of twenty-six and that he was more of a source of wisdom when forty-five.

"Quinton, have we been in each other's lives before?" Quinton said we had tried it before, meaning that he had left early. We were doing it again because we hadn't gotten it the first time. I got the sense that the comment was directed toward me and that I hadn't gotten it the first time. Quinton added that he was a kindred soul and that words couldn't show the true bond between us.

"Have you seen your grandpas?" Quinton's response was interesting. He replied, "Yes and never. I saw them as I came through." He continued by saying one of them was fishing by a lake; the other was still connected to quite a few people and was lending his energy to help them. This was a profound statement. Quinton had never known my father, and Leianne knew neither, but the statement was spot on. My father was the fisherman; he was the grandpa fishing by a lake. My father-in-law was the grandpa who was still nearby helping those of his family who needed him.

"Quinton, was your leaving us part of your soul contract?" For those of you not acquainted with soul contracts, there is a school of thought that believes, upon birth, all of us have intended experiences and that within those experiences are tasks we are to complete. These tasks may very well relate to an impact upon others. The experiences and tasks make up our soul contracts. Further embedded within our contracts, we will usually find obstacles or habits that we must work toward overcoming. Quinton answered the question, "Yes and executed quite succinctly." He added that there was sadness when he left; he felt bad about what he was leaving behind, but his spirit guides reminded him of his contract. Quinton wanted to remind us that our lives here are about the experience and not the destination. A comment in my journal says "like bro/brothers, comrades in arms; ritual." I don't know if this comment was describing Quinton's and my relationship or Quinton and Cheyanne's relationship. Although it was Quinton and Cheyanne in the first reading, this time it felt like Quinton and me.

"Quinton, why did you get out of the Suburban?" He said, "I was instructed . . . no logic or reason."

As we finished, Quinton added that I would see him again in a different but similar form. He shared again that he can shadow or superimpose himself onto others (referring to piggybacking) and that it was important to see him as an adult. Quinton added, "Say hello to Mom" and mentioned the image of a poppy flower in connection with her. The message was that Quinton would send Kristine one image of a poppy flower. Quinton's last comment in that session was "It is amazing to see reality from my perspective. I can see all realities, potential realities, and lived realities."

Then we were done.

It is probably important to point out that I typically don't ask a lot of additional questions relating to my original questions during these sessions. I let Quinton lead, because I have faith that the information I need to hear will be imparted. In addition, I don't want to appear needy or desperate to stay in contact, in part because I know that I can have direct contact with Quinton just by thinking of him or asking for him to visit.

Chapter Twelve

QUINTON'S MESSAGES

Quinton's messages are succinct and as clear as he lived them. While they are succinct and clear to us, it isn't that he told us or channeled them directly to us after he transitioned. I still struggle to live for myself, the near-perfect example of the very information he was born to impart to his family and all those with whom he came in contact.

Quinton was born with this knowledge as I have come to believe all children do. He didn't learn it from a book, school, or even his parents, although we provided an environment that allowed him to keep the knowledge and innocence he was born with. Maybe he is impacting some of your lives as you read this book, even though you have never met him. Quinton clearly lived to help everyone he came in contact with, not expecting anything in return, and he did so while enjoying life. How many of us are able to live this way?

Quinton demonstrated that he was in the physical realm to provide support to the people in need with whom he came into direct contact. He was always so considerate and caring to everyone. He was always quick with a smile or to offer comfort. He never ridiculed others or put them down, though that is done so often by people desperate to make themselves feel better and do so at somebody else's expense. When an individual was mean to him, Quinton never retaliated, but in his hurt, he would ask, "Why?" While he never did figure that out, he didn't let it dampen his spirit. That was the first message to all of us: help one another without expectation. Let's help each other while in the state of love and kindness, not in a state of anger or intimidation. In other words, like our son, let's be there for one another from a state of love and not loathing.

Quinton played like he knew he would be leaving us early. During the summer months, he loved being outside and would play with his friends next door until he was exhausted, and then he would keep playing. When Quinton played, he would forget to eat, and when he was little, he would often forget to go the bathroom (oops). Our last vacation together was no different. He vacationed on Lake Powell like there would not be another vacation; in fact, he vacationed like there would not be a tomorrow. He was always in the water and was annoyed with us if at least one of us wasn't in there with him. That was the second message to all of us: enjoy your time with one another. Play and have fun; be grateful for your time in the physical realm; be grateful for each breath you breathe, each tear, each smile, and each laugh!

Quinton's last message was an implied message, for you see, many have sensed Quinton in one way or another since he returned to a state of pure energy. I have seen him and heard him call my name. He has come to me and others in visions and in dreams. In these visions, he has let us know that he was okay. In my case, Quinton let me know that he was with me at all times! Quinton came to a friend of mine at the service, one of his aunts, some of his cousins, friends, and the list goes on.

As we talked and shared, invariably we ended up visiting with others who had suffered losses. Something unexpected has come from those conversations. The vast majority of those we have spoken with have sensed their transitioned loved ones as well or know of others who have heard from their transitioned loved ones. We shared our experiences, because they were ours and nobody could take them away from us. All the while, we knew some might not believe us. When we shared our experiences, the people we shared with would often share their experiences with us, because they knew they wouldn't be ridiculed. The third message was a spiritual message: There is more to our existence than our physical bodies, and we continue to exist once we leave our physical bodies. Quinton still is, and all of our transitioned loved ones are. It blew me away and certainly put our lives here within our bags of flesh into a different perspective and context. I, for one, am reading everything I can get my hands on to learn more and am constantly amazed by how much knowledge that speaks to this truth that is available.

The grandest message of them all is, life is truly eternal; all of us are eternal beings. It isn't some and not others – all of us are eternal. Whether we go to church or not; whether we pray or not; whether we are "good" or "bad", whatever good or bad truly means. All of us are eternal. And with this knowledge, will you look at your time here any differently? This is a divine message, one for all of us. This is an invitation to look at our lives and our struggles differently.

It is this information that we have come to understand as messages. Given that both Kristine and I survived the accident only through the grace of God, we believe that we must continue to share, so you, dear reader, can have the benefit of knowing Quinton as we did. In a way, we are keeping him alive to the benefit of as many people as possible.

Chapter Thirteen

WHAT HAPPENS WHEN OUR LOVED ONES TRANSITION

This section of the book can easily be a book in itself, given how much material has already been published by so many others. I am including this section in our book because what we experienced and what almost everyone who has shared with us has experienced appears not to be common knowledge. Why? Everyone should know—or remember to be more accurate—that there is more to us than these bodies in which we currently reside.

How is it that we didn't know? How is it that nobody told us? Why wasn't this common knowledge? Why isn't this taught in schools or shared on TV, in the newspapers, and on the Internet every day? Why does our western society keep us totally in the dark regarding the simple fact that there is more to us than meets the eye? Does the reality that we still exist when we leave our physical bodies undermine society's hold on us? It sure seems that way. Otherwise, this would be known by all. I imagine it is possible that only I didn't know, given that I hadn't spent a lot of time in church during my life, but this scenario is unlikely. The point here is, church shouldn't be the only place where this knowledge is available.

Can you imagine a world in which all of us know our true selves as a divine energy or as Christ's spark and that we still exist after we leave our physical bodies, after we transition? All of a sudden, all of the silliness that we think is important would cease to be important—all the drama, all the news, all the fads, all of it! We could laugh at it all, relinquish society's hold on us, and not let its negative energy bring us down. All of a sudden, we would cease to be afraid of one another. We would look each other in the eye, and know that we are communicating with others who have a divine spark of energy, just like us.

Wouldn't that be amazing? Can you imagine that place? Well, it is here for many of us There is a school of thought that the best of us are being called home (a.k.a. transitioning to pure energy or, if that is still too hard to digest, dying) and doing so because they can do more for us from the other side. Wow—yes, there is more to our reality than the silly little noises emitted by our society every day. Can you imagine a time and place in which all of us know this? Once we do, we will inherently recognize that we are okay, and the need to compete with each other for energy will cease entirely. As that occurs, we suddenly realize that the only reason we have that big house or big car, that newest gadget, those fancy clothes, or work so hard at being the "fairest of all" is because we are just trying to be okay. Our society has set us up, on some level, to compete with one another for our own self-esteem. Can you imagine if that all stopped? I can, and I bet others can too. Those who pull the strings can imagine it all too well.

That is where we, Kristine and I, found ourselves at that point. None of these excuses were important. Our beloved son, Quinton, was called home in a manner that felt preordained, and then he continued to visit us. Now that was reality. We no longer watched the news, because we saw it for what it was: noise or worse, a system designed to fill us with negative energy and make us afraid of one another. I can't help but ask, "Why does such a system exist?" If we all woke up and realized who we were, we could stop competing for an unlimited resource, our own spirituality and energy.

As the veil thinned and we began to see through the illusion of our reality today, we stopped buying stuff that we didn't need. We stopped trying to find our happiness through simply buying; many of us have everything we need—essentials and nonessentials—but we keep buying just to feel good about ourselves, if only for only a moment. When the moment is over, we feel dissatisfied with ourselves all over again. That is the bottom line: if we stopped buying and spending to only feel good, our economy would be tilted up on its axis, which, I am afraid, is why we have been intentionally misled. But more and more of us are waking up.

With the transition of our son in the forefront of our minds and in the minds of the people closest to us, we awoke. Were we alone? Not at all. We had been in contact with so many of our friends and neighbors in our mountain community who had had similar experiences. That in just a little mountain town of fifteen thousand people or so; can you imagine speaking to everyone in America or the world and hearing of their experiences? There is a wealth of material that speaks of this suddenly larger reality that we were coming to know.

Joe and Ann Kecter

I began to realize that others shared our experience when Joe and Ann Kecter came by our home during the summer of 2009. It was probably August. They came by with their daughter Ashley to pick up Cheyanne to go and do something fun, to take Cheyanne's mind off Quinton's death. They knew exactly what they were doing, because they too knew death, unfortunately. Their son, Matt, died during the Columbine incident in 1999.

I was outside working on our deck project when Joe walked up to me. With a twinkle in his blue eyes, he leaned close and asked, "Have you seen anything strange?" What courage that took to ask that simple open-ended question. How could he have known how I might respond? I excitedly said, "Yes." To which he replied, "Enjoy it, because it won't last forever." While we didn't discuss any more on that occasion, I expected we would do so soon. Joe was the first to really open my eyes to the fact that others had experiences like we were having. That was huge!

Bob and Mary Beaty

I had known Bob and Mary Beaty since attending Evergreen High School from the fall of 1980 to the spring of 1983. Bob was our head football coach, and Mary was his wife. In November of 2008, I was fortunate to visit with Bob during his last week in the physical realm. I hadn't seen Bob since the mid-eighties, and I was ashamed that so much time had passed. Alex Brister had called me with the bad news that Bob was in the advanced stage of prostate cancer. Alex and I went down there together. I think both of us were afraid of what we would see.

Bob and Mary welcomed us into their home. Mary jumped into my arms like I was family. For a second, I was confused, because Bob was walking around looking as fit as a fiddle, but I soon realized that was his son Shaun who looked just like him. Bob was on the couch and frail but beaming with love.

The night was special. We told stories and reminisced. Doug Wills and Kent Waryan were there, along with others whom I didn't know. After two or three hours, I noticed concern on the faces of Mary and her daughter, Cindy; Bob was fatigued. I stood up to leave, as did most of the visitors. One week later on November 14, Bob transitioned. Afterward, Mary shared, "We spoke of you often during those years we were not in contact, and Bob was always concerned about where life had taken you. It was Providence that brought us together. Bob and I were so pleased to see you and the other very special people who came to see him. Those visits were an affirmation of his life."

During the winter of 2010—I think it was February—Kristine and I had brunch with Mary. We had an amazing visit, and she demonstrated how well she knew me. She knew more of my home life than I had realized. Mary illustrated this by reminiscing of the time she sat on her deck having lunch with me while I was on break from a work-detail crew made up of football players. We were there working on a deck expansion at their home on a part-time basis while on summer break from high school classes. I didn't remember the deck expansion or the conversation, but apparently intimated some of our difficult home life. I did remember another summer when we were installing railroad ties along their driveway in Evergreen. My memory is so finicky, which is the price of blocking out the ugliness of my childhood. I lost some of the good memories too.

Our conversation turned to the reason I had asked to visit with her. We began speaking of metaphysics and quantum physics. I shared my enjoyment of Joseph Campbell's *The Power of Myth,* and she excitedly told me that she used that very book while teaching. She shared that, as Bob and Mary realized that he would lose his battle to prostate cancer, a friend advised them that they should see a nearby psychologist, who was intuitive. Without going into too many personal details of those sessions, I can say that, near the end, the doctor asked Bob how he would make his presence known after he transitioned to pure energy. Bob replied that he would mess with the therapist's lights; and he has. I asked Mary if she had sensed him in any way, and she replied that he had come to her with a big smile in a vision.

Mary and Todd Gilmer

Kristine, Quinton, Cheyanne, and I had known the Gilmers for about eight years. Cheyanne and their daughter, Gloria, attended elementary, middle, and high school together. They played soccer together until high school, which was where we spent most of our time with them. We all had fond memories of attending the girls' soccer games. Quinton would often climb into the middle of the tandem foldout chair we brought to the games or climb into its carrying case.

Mary and Todd were there for us after Quinton transitioned. Mary made a collage containing the obituary and prayer card, and Todd spent time with me as I shared the larger reality that I had become aware of. After one of our visits during the summer of 2009, when I shared the larger picture of reality that Quinton revealed to us, Todd said, "You are living an adventure." He said so with love, awe, and admiration. Little did he know that he and Mary would be doing the same in the not-too-distant future.

On February 6, 2010, Mary and Todd lost their middle son, Alex, in an airplane accident over Boulder, Colorado. It devastated them. Alex, a marine who fought in Iraq, was back in the States working as a pilot when, while he was towing a glider, another plane flew into him. He never had a chance.

I went to comfort Todd as best I could, just as Todd had come to me. During that first visit, neither Mary nor Todd mentioned seeing any signs from Alex, but their friends shared a couple of interesting accounts.

Alex was witnessed in the hanger where he used to be based moments after the accident. When an individual saw Alex with the understanding that he could not possibly be there, the individual knew something was amiss and surmised that there had been an accident.

Alex's cousin Debbie, who lived in Minnesota, suddenly burst into tears for no apparent reason at the moment when Alex was called home. She had spent three years training her dog, Jasmine, not to get on the bed, but at that moment, she grabbed Jasmine, lifted her to the bed, and sobbed into her softness for hours. Much later in the day when she received a phone call and was informed of the bad news. How was that possible? Coincidence? Again, it is easy to say it is until it happens to you.

In subsequent conversations with Mary in the summer of 2010, she revealed that Alex had been visiting her in her dreams, which like Quinton's visits to me, were crystal clear, as if they weren't a dream at all but a vision. One in particular moved her to follow Alex's instruction and take action. In her vision, Alex and Mary were in the car together, as they often were while he was growing up. Much as he had done while in the physical realm, he gently reminded her of something she was forgetting. Her vision continued, and as they sat in the car, he kept hinting that she was forgetting something.

In 2007, Alex saved the life of his friend. They had been hang gliding when his friend hit dead air and plummeted to the ground. Alex was behind him and quickly landed, called 911, and administered CPR until emergency crews could land. In Mary's vision, Alex directed her to check on his friend and see how he was doing (it was three years later), which she did.

If you want to know more about Alex, please go to www. AlexGilmerScholarship.org.

Leianne Wilson

On November 21, 2007, Leianne's close friend, John, transitioned. She was separated from him when he passed, but she almost immediately realized that John was visiting in spirit every evening. She was numb. His passing made for a very dismal holiday season, and she grieved deeply for the emptiness of lost love. Fortunately, her family was there to help her during her difficult time. Her brother helped her put up the Christmas tree while visiting, even though her heart wasn't in it. When her brother's visit ended and she was in the house alone again, she noticed that John's presence was greatly magnified. It was easy to know his messages and communications; sometimes he would rub her crown chakra, which left a distinct tingling on her head. To her surprise and delight, sometimes he caressed her cheek, leaving a physical sensation that verified his presence. Every evening for the whole holiday season, she sat and conversed with him, feeling his closeness.

When January rolled around, she decided it was time to take down the holiday decorations. She immediately noticed that, while she could still hear and feel him, those sensations were significantly weaker. It didn't take long for John to intimate to her that he had been drawing energy from the Christmas lights; now that they had been taken down, he had less energy to work with. He got his message across by firmly putting the image of a ficus tree covered in lights into Leianne's head. Leianne heeded the message, went to the store, bought two big ficus trees, decorated them up with lights, and was able to continue sensing him afterward.

John continued to visit for some time, but eventually his visits became less frequent. Although they were less frequent, he still show up when Leianne was in difficult situations. It took Leianne three or four times to make the connection, but she learned that, when she felt his caress on her cheek, she understood it as a warning of sorts. She knew she needed an immediate change of scenery.

John McDonough

My friend, John McDonough, told me this story three times, and I know it is intended to be included here. Many years ago, John's friend, Hal Maw, passed away suddenly in a single-car accident on a blue-sky afternoon. Sometime before Hal's transition, John and Hal had been out to the local bar; John had driven. Hal realized that he had a pipe in his pocket, and he didn't want to bring it into the club. He placed it in the glove box of John's car and forgot to retrieve it when John dropped him off later. For months afterward, John never saw the pipe, even though he had been in his glove box several times.

On the day after Hal transitioned, John received a card from a woman who would soon be his wife that featured a *Far Side* comic. In the cartoon image, two deer were standing together, and one deer said to the other deer, "Bummer of a birthmark, Hal"; the birthmark was a perfect bull's-eye target on its chest. An hour later, as John read the local paper, a name jumped out from a section he didn't usually read—the obituary section. It was Hal Maw, which was not a common name; John realized then that he had transitioned. Later that same day, as he was still in shock at the news, he needed to get something from his car and entered from the passenger side. When he opened his glove box, there was Hal's pipe, sitting in plain view.

Those three powerful incidents occurred in one day, but the icing on the cake came one evening a week later when John and his friends, who were also Hal's friends, sat on a Florida beach one evening and toasted Hal by offering his favorite cocktail, a Sea Breeze, to the Gulf of Mexico as each of them took a sip of his own beverage. At the exact moment they toasted Hal, each lifting his respective drink to the sky, a bolt of spider lighting filled the sky above. John and his friends all looked at each other and knew Hal was there with them and making his presence known.

As if that wasn't a clear enough message for them, a month later the same group of friends with a few more sat on the beach on the Fourth of July enjoying the many firework displays up and down the beach. It was a gorgeous evening with perfect weather and great friends. After all of the shows had long been wrapped up, the comment was made, "The only thing that could have made this evening more perfect would be if Hal had been here with us." Almost before the words had been said, a shooting star streaked across the night sky. Looking at each other, each wondered if he had imagined it, but it was seen by most of the group. Once again, Hal had reached out to let them know he was still around.

Sandrena Brockman Robinson and Daniel Brockman

Sandrena was very close to her dad, Daniel Brockman. She shared with me that, when he transitioned, a part of her died with him. She had been separated from her father for more than eight years. Unbeknownst to both of them, this time period would represent the last eight years of his life. However, it would also be an awe-inspiring eight years as he chose to leave the United States to work as the chief pharmacist at Phoebe Pharmaceutical and Nursing School, located 116 miles up-country from Monrovia, Liberia, in West Africa.

During those years, Sandrena's biggest frustration came from contacting him by phone. Often she would awaken early in the morning and begin calling without hope of getting through until late afternoon. This was primarily due to the inadequate telecommunication systems throughout the rural areas of Liberia. Fortunately for her, he would take a break from the mission for three months during the summer of each year. During those three-month breaks, he spent a month traveling throughout Africa or Europe and two months at his home in the States. On one occasion, Sandrena took a sabbatical from work to travel with him to four African countries. His visits to his home in the United States always lasted sixty days. At the end of each visit, Sandrena would beg him to stay just one more day, and he would reply, "Sorry, sweetheart, but I have stayed one day longer than I was supposed to."

During the seventh year of his mission, the family was dealt a devastating blow when Sandrena's oldest sister, Karen Brockman

Williams, was diagnosed with stage-four breast cancer. Daniel decided to come home that Christmas instead of that summer so that he could spend the holidays with his girls. It was during that visit that he purchased more than two hundred wrist watches as gifts for his staff and persons in his care at the mission hospital on the Phoebe compound. He feared that he would never get them through customs and was reluctant about mailing them, because mail service was extremely slow. Sandrena purchased a travel bag for him and he got them through customs without a problem.

Karen learned that she had cancer on November 15, Sandrena's birthday. It couldn't have been a sadder moment for the two of them and the family in general. Just before the Thanksgiving holidays, she had a mastectomy. Daniel was happy to be by her side. Oddly, in spite of the chemotherapy and radiation and besides losing her hair, she never looked sick a day in her life. However, Daniel was not looking well. Everyone notice that he looked really tired, but they brushed it off thinking he was tired and just really worried about Karen. Daniel didn't have the heart to tell them he too had cancer—pancreatic cancer. He came home one last time on April 14, 1989 and transitioned to pure energy on June 15, 1989, sixty-one days after his last arrival. Before he transitioned, he told Sandrena three things: don't marry Wiley (Sandrena's first husband, to whom she was engaged to at the time) stating "If you do, you'll be miserable for as long as you remain his wife as your family values are very different"; "Don't live life based upon material things as they will not bring you happiness"; and "In the end, the truth will be known." His last words were haunting for Sandrena, because she knew those were promises she would not keep. Three days after sharing those words of wisdom, he transitioned.

Right after Daniel passed away, Sandrena knew that she had to inform the people who had become his second family in Africa, his coworkers, and his friends. She prepared to spend hours trying to get through on the phone. Not only did she get through on the first attempt, but she got through on the first ring, much to her surprise. As Sandrena put it, it was the first sign that her father was there with her, helping her to do what she needed to do. It was her responsibility to settle the affairs of both of his estates—the one in Africa and the one in the United States.

On the eve of her departure for New York, her father came to her. Sandrena wasn't feeling well and was lying in bed, waiting for sleep to come, when suddenly it seemed as if a light had been turned on. She saw her father. He appeared sick, but when Sandrena called "Daddy," he suddenly looked healthy again. It was then that he told her, "You're going to be okay." The room darkened and Sandrena's dad was gone. Sandrena truly believes she saw her father, and firmly states that "Nothing of this earth will ever make me believe I did not see him!"

Against the advice of her father, she married Wiley in New York while they were on their way to Africa, and they honeymooned in Amsterdam. The second sign came on the last day of her honeymoon as she stood in the airport in Morocco after a plane change following their flight from Amsterdam. A priest came over to compliment her beautiful smile. During their conversation, he asked where Sandrena and Wiley were going. Sandrena replied that they were going to Monrovia, Liberia, to memorialize her father who had recently passed away. Without pause, the priest said, "Oh my, you're Danny's daughter; I should have known from the smile." Sandrena cried, because she knew she wasn't alone. Her Pooh Bear, as she had affectionately called her father, was with her once again.

The third sign came on the day of the service that was conducted for him in Phoebe, which happened to occur during the African monsoon season. Although it had been raining heavily for an entire week, the rain suddenly stopped before the service was to begin, and the sun came out. Sandrena shared that, in Africa, those attending a funeral would take their emotional cue from the grieving family. Remember those watches? At 2:00 p.m. sharp, the alarms on two hundred or more watches all began to chime. Everyone whom Daniel had given a watch to was there in attendance, but no one had known how to change the alarms. Sandrena started to giggle when she realized what was happening, and the entire congregation did the same, except they didn't know or understand why they were smiling and, in some cases, laughing.

As Sandrena and her husband packed her father's belongings, she found a letter he had written to God exactly one year prior to that day. This was the fourth sign of her father's presence. In the letter, he had asked God to watch over his loved ones and thanked God for the opportunity to serve so many in West Africa. He also asked for forgiveness if he had wronged anyone. More importantly, he asked God to protect Sandrena and her sister Rushane and their mother Vivian from disease. He stated, "I'm not asking for my beloved Karen, for I know she will be all right." This was very odd, because this letter was written on August 17, 1988, and Karen was not diagnosed with breast cancer until November 15, 1988. Sandrena wondered how her father could have known, and then she interpreted the letter to mean that Karen would be okay. She never expected her sister to die thirteen months later. But somehow her father had known she would. In the end, the truth will be known.

Sandrena Brockman Wilson and Karen Brockman

For those of you who are struggling to grasp what is being illustrated by these personal accounts, you will really get a charge out of this one. Karen transitioned on her favorite holiday, July 4, in 1990. As stated earlier, even though she succumbed to cancer, she never looked sick a day in her life. Karen knew that Sandrena had always wanted a little girl. So before her passing she told Sandrena that, if it was the last thing she did, she was going to see to it that Sandrena would receive the gift of a daughter. Karen always felt bad that her announcement of having cancer came on Sandrena's birthday. So she constantly said, "When I get to heaven, I'm going to see to it that you get your little girl." Sandrena didn't like her sister's suggestion that she might die, so she refused to listen to her rambles about making sure Sandrena received her wish. Karen was so adamant about it that that she told her first cousin, Rosetta Griffin, as well. Sandrena learned of that after she adopted McKenna.

Sandrena and Wiley had been trying to have a child without much luck. So Wiley wanted Sandrena to consider various fertility methods. Sandrena has always been petrified of needles because she had been so sick as a child and had had three major operations before the age of five. She wouldn't consider anything other than adoption. They talked to many other people who had similar fertility problems and had chosen adoption. While on a company ski trip, Sandrena spent a lot of time talking with a fellow real-estate broker and friend named Marc who had adopted a little girl. Amazingly, his adopted daughter looked exactly like him, even though he was not her biological father. Then Marc introduced Sandrena to a couple who had adopted two biracial boys and knew that their adoption agency was looking for a qualified African American family to adopt a little girl. Background checks were performed, and the agency conducted a home study to make sure Sandrena's home was a suitable environment.

On April 9, which was Good Friday, Sandrena met Iris Star Glen-Bacon for the first time. Star, as she was called before Sandrena and Wiley renamed her McKenna Danielle Wilson, was eight months old when she arrived at their home. Before the placement, Sandrena and Wiley decided not to mention to anyone that they were considering adopting her in fear that it might not happen. Much to their astonishment, Joloni (Karen's son who was eleven years old then but had been only nine when his mom died) called one evening to announce that he knew his cousin. Sandrena politely asked him what he was referring to. He said, "Star. They call her Star . . . you know, the little baby that you are going to adopt." Sandrena asked how he knew about that. He said that Star's foster mom was a friend of the woman who was dating his father at the time. He also shared that he played with her every Saturday when his father's girlfriend took him to play basketball at the recreation center in Park Hill. As you might imagine, Sandrena was filled with emotion as Joloni ended his story by saying, "Auntie, I prayed over Star [McKenna] every Saturday. I wanted her to find a nice mommy and daddy, since she lost her mommy too! I'm glad she found you."

On May 1, McKenna became part of Sandrena and Wiley's family. That was the same day Sandrena hosted a baby shower for her sister Rushane. McKenna seemed amazed by all of the people, maybe a little scared too! She sat quietly in her father's lap, sucking her thumb. When

Joloni arrived, she became wide-eyed and started babbling and reaching out for him. His was the only face she knew.

One night, after McKenna was just a bit older than three, she woke up crying. Sandrena rushed into her room to see what had caused her to awaken so upset. McKenna just kept saying she was hungry. Sandrena couldn't imagine why she would be, but she asked her if she wanted something to drink. McKenna replied "No, I want French fries!" Sandrena said she almost fainted, because, to her knowledge, McKenna had never eaten French fries. Wiley was quite adamant that his child would not be brought up eating McDonalds. What made it so shocking was that French fries had been Karen's favorite food. Sandrena knew at that moment that her sister had kept her promise.

Strange occurrences still transpire. Maybe the strangest of all was that, when McKenna arrived at Sandrena's home, she was a very fair-complexioned African American baby. Her skin tone remained that way for years. As she reached her teenage years, her pigment and features have changed as it does with many children. Oddly, McKenna now looks exactly like Karen (and Sandrena has pictures that bear witness of this fact). Sandrena contends that McKenna has Karen's body shape, her smile, and most of all her disposition.

Karen was born on September 21, 1951, and McKenna was born September 3, 1992. I guess if you were into numerology, you could suggest that there is a correlation; if you add the two and the one in Karen's birth date together, you get three, which is the number of McKenna's birth date. Oh well, stranger things have happened, I suppose.

Ed Cano and Quinton S. Jackson

Quinton and his grandfather, Ed Cano, had a special, albeit brief, relationship. Quinton was three and a half years old when Ed passed away, but while they were both with us, Ed usually called every morning to speak with Quinton, who looked forward to speaking with "Papa." Not long after Ed transitioned on July 8, 2003, Quinton shared with the family that he had an imaginary friend named Cardo. The obvious connection was that Cardo was in fact Ed, due to the timing of Cardo's arrival. While it wasn't obvious then, as we look back and remember, Cardo's arrival was within six months of Ed's departure. Yes, I know that many children have imaginary friends. In fact, it is safe to say that all of us either know a child with an imaginary friend or know of a child with an imaginary friend.

I was decidedly unenlightened at that point in my life, so I may have heard mention of Cardo, but I didn't pay any attention. Cheyanne paid attention and would ask Quinton, "Who is Cardo?" to which Quinton would reply, "He is my friend." I was still fully engrossed in the illusion of life that our society has us so fully immersed within. While I can't say I didn't believe it, I can say that I didn't pay any attention; rarely was it mentioned around me. In fact, I don't think Quinton mentioned his friend to me once, even though they spent time together for at least three years. One day, Kristine asked Quinton about his friend, and he replied that he had left.

How often do parents squash thoughts of imaginary friends? It has only been since Quinton transitioned that I have learned the true nature of most imaginary friends in the multitude of books I have been reading. Children often see things that we don't. I can remember both of my children staring off into space with big grins on their faces when they were toddlers, and I forever wondered what they were seeing; I never even considered that they were seeing through the veil separating the physical and nonphysical. Interestingly and probably not surprisingly, almost all children reach a point when their imaginary friends either go away or they no longer see them. I wish I had known this when my children were toddlers. Needless to say, I am drawn to children more than ever as I share my energy and feel theirs in return. There is nothing in the world like a child's smile; I wonder what they are seeing that I cannot.

Ryan Nicholson

I have already shared the role Cathie and Troy Nicholson played in our lives; both of them had huge impacts. Ryan was four years younger than Quinton, and he played an almost equally large role. Ryan saw the world a little bit differently. He walked to his own drum beat and could keep himself entertained for hours. Just like Quinton, he too could play for hours by himself and with others. I never knew what to expect from him because sometimes he was so focused upon what he was doing that he didn't notice me, and other times, he gave me such a warm embrace that I thought Quinton had joined him in hugging me.

Q and Ryan at Halloween

Ryan had an imaginary friend, except she wasn't so imaginary after all. Cathie was a friend and neighbor of Mike and Desiree Watcher. They had celebrated each other's weddings and spent a lot of time together. Desiree and Cathie were pregnant at the same time and enjoyed many fun times together as new life grew within them. Ryan was born only a few weeks before Melina. Unfortunately, Melina became sick; she transitioned when she was ten months old after contracting and battling infant acute lymphoblastic leukemia. Her diagnosis and passing led Cathie to become a volunteer for the Leukemia and Lymphoma Society where she worked several years,

Not long after Melina transitioned, Troy and Cathie put Ryan to bed in his crib. When they checked on him a little bit later, he was giggling. They asked him what he was doing, and he told them he was playing with Angel Mia. He called her Mia because he could not pronounce Melina. They asked Ryan where Angel Mia was and he pointed to the skylight. She would often play with Ryan in his room, and he was very forward about her existence. Both Troy and Cathie understood the significance of Ryan's imaginary friend, and neither of them denied him his friend.

Mara Parslow

On January 5, 2010, Mara Parslow of Conifer, Colorado, transitioned in a traffic accident at Shaffer's Crossing between Pine Junction and Conifer. There were three Conifer High School students in the vehicle, and Cheyanne knew all of them. It was a horrific accident that took the lives of Mara and Kenneth Barnett.

Later that spring, Kathy White, whose son Brad had been dating Mara, reached out to Kristine. She asked if we would be willing to speak with Cathee Lecount, Mara's mom, because many in the community were amazed by how well we were after Quinton's transition. We were more than willing. Kristine and I spoke with Cathee often in March and April of 2010. I shared my reading list with her, and we discussed the books that we read while she shared with us that she had seen evidence of Mara's presence.

As the writing of this book continued to progress during the summer of the 2010, I called her and asked if she would be willing to meet and discuss her experiences with Mara. We met on July 24, and I was struck by how much Mara and her mother looked alike. During the visit when I met her son Jeffrey, daughter Autumn, and cocker spaniel Lady-Bug, Cathee shared that there was a picture of Mara on her bureau, and next to it was one of Mara's favorite bracelets. The bracelet was always set up flush against the picture. Cathleen checked it in the evening when she went to bed, and in the morning, the bracelet had been moved. This went on for days after Mara transitioned to pure energy; there was no logical explanation other than that Mara was doing it from a nonphysical realm. There is more, but this account is hard to dispute even for the most skeptical.

Often, the books Cathee and I had read directed us to be mindful and pay attention. We should look at everything going on around us for signs that our transitioned loved ones were trying to contact us using anything from what might seem like odd behavior in the wildlife to a special song popping up. That very thing happened to Cathee on more than one occasion. For a specific example, right after reminiscing about Mara, she picked up Mara's iPod and suddenly Elkand's song "Apart" was playing. The first line to the song is, "You and I will never be apart." Pay attention.

We continue to be in contact with Cathee.

Not long after our visit, she went to San Diego. While there, she asked Mara to send her a sign to let her know she was with them. One day, Cathee was in a gift shop and her sister texted her, asking to meet. When she picked up her phone, a picture of Mara and her was on the screen.

"Funny," Cathee shared, "You'd have to push at least five buttons to get from the main screen to where that picture is. But you and I know who was responsible for that. It gives me so much strength to know she is still with me and able to send me signs. Just thought I'd share that with you."

And the beat goes on.

Angel

On April 21, 2010, I stopped at a car wash just outside of Evergreen. While there, I noticed a young mother and her adorable daughter. The precocious child was eighteen months old. She was full of joy as she played in the car wash lobby. I ended up playing catch with her. Her Mom's name was Angel, and she saw how I was drawn to her daughter and asked if I had children. I told her I had Cheyanne, who was sixteen at the time, and Quinton, who was pure energy.

Angel shared that her married friend had lost an eighteen-month-old daughter and their older son of three years old could see her, but this so frightened the young parents that they were doing everything in their power to dissuade him from the visions. I became exasperated, and I explained that he really was seeing her. Angel agreed, but her friends didn't get it yet. They were afraid.

Chris Erickson

"My story . . . it is firsthand.

"My stepfather was a force of nature. He owned a very lucrative local construction company here in Colorado. He loved my mother dearly, and I adored him. He died in July seventeen years ago. He told my mother prior to his death that, if it was possible, he would come back and watch after her.

"Approximately five months after he died, I was at my mom's for dinner and to help put up Christmas decorations. As we were getting dinner ready, the Tupperware lid on the pitcher kept popping up; we would shut it, and it would pop up again. What was funny was that it was hard to open or close it. I teased her and told her that my stepfather was playing with her, and we smiled, reminisced, and sat down to dinner.

"As we started cleaning the dishes, we heard a sound upstairs. It upset us, because we were the only ones in the house. We looked for the noise and finally recognized the sound as a music box or something similar. We opened the door to my stepfather's old closet, and there sat the teddy bear my mom had given him. It had a red heart with the words 'I love you' that lit up and played music. We always put it out with the Xmas decorations, but it was in his closet and not with the Xmas decorations.

"We believe he was saying 'I still love you!' Of course, we both cried our eyes out and made sure the bear was put out with the decorations.

"The next year, I was again at the house helping set up for Xmas, the same musical sounds came from the same closet and bear. Mom looked almost green; she said, 'I took the batteries out of the bear last year.' We opened it, and sure enough, there were no batteries. I don't think that I have ever felt so loved as in the moment.

"Some people who knew him think that it could happen, but most people I have spoken to have come up with reasons why this could have happened (i.e., batteries were old and just surged, or there were still traces of battery carbon left—all kinds of speculation). Others just don't believe. However, they don't have to; I know and feel the love that he gave us on these occasions.

"It has been many years now, but both my mom and I seem to have dreams. Often we have them at the same time. We always call each other and are always amazed that we were thinking of him at the same time. I know he is there and is looking out for the family still.

"This is my story. Of course, I am crying typing it; it always brings a smile to me and sadness that he isn't here with us now. But I know that we were and are loved very much."

How do you explain these incidents to those who haven't had such experiences? How do we explain these experiences to people who are skeptical, whose rational minds are filled with a passed-down knowledge that often isn't based upon reality? Many don't share for fear of being ridiculed or thought of as odd. For those of us who do share, we share not only because we believe what we have seen, heard, felt, and witnessed but because we knew that all of it was real—just as real as, if not more so, than the fabric of our society that continues to wrap us in an illusion. Nonbelievers attempt to punch holes in our accounts, but someday they themselves will sense something that defies their belief systems, and then perhaps they will begin to see the larger picture. For those of us who have lost loved ones, we share with those we are comfortable sharing with. For me, I will share with everybody I can. Quinton's visits to us are far too significant for us not to share or, so much worse, for us to forget. But it doesn't end. It continues and will continue with everyone who shares personal experiences with us.

Quinton's Messages

Recently, we were at a barbeque, and an acquaintance named Nancy shared her account of a squirrel making a sudden appearance, which very much reminded us of the hummingbird's behaviors during the summer of 2009. In the home of a relative who had suffered the second of two completely unexpected family transitions exactly one year apart from each other, the actions of a squirrel made them all take notice. After the funeral service, the family gathered in the living room. Outside the living room was a deck with no rail. The window overlooking the deck only had a narrow piece of wood trim on the outside, yet somehow a squirrel was suddenly perched with its face on the window. It was looking in at them with no rational explanation, but they all knew what was going on, as do those of us who have experienced similar unusual behavior from nature's animals.

Chapter Fourteen

WHO WE WERE

As part of the editing process of *Quinton's Messages*, I shared a very rough manuscript with some of those mentioned within the book. As I met with each of them afterward, I volunteered to some that I was going to remove this section entirely on the basis that the energy associated with the telling of my life didn't fit with Quinton's energy. I was met with a resounding no. My friends asserted that the telling of who I was would be important because it illustrated that I wasn't necessarily an individual making my way through life on the cusp of being enlightened.

I included this section initially, because I have felt as if I was in a bubble during my entire life, protected from what was truly an awful existence; that bubble was not of my own making. I felt that I was protected by God or a guardian angel, so I could survive relatively untainted and, in hindsight, do what I am doing now: write a book and testify to our experiences. For me, it fits, so here goes.

Ernie Jackson

I was born on December 12, 1964, to Frances Ernell Jackson and Ernest James Jackson. Both of my parents experienced difficult lives that clearly molded me into the individual that I am.

My mother was conceived in South Hill, Virginia, when her mom, Dorothy Jackson, went to the shoe store in 1943. She did not have money, and the owner of the store took sex from Dorothy for payment. I have no idea how this interaction went, but I do know that my mom was born as a direct result. Maybe that was the norm out there in the woods of southern Virginia. Despite that auspicious start to her life and the fact that she was the lightest colored member of the family, Mom lived a good and happy life until her Mom remarried and her stepfather began raping her when she was thirteen. This abuse continued. Her mother refused to believe it was happening, and therefore, she did nothing about it. Still my mom went back to Virginia and took care of her mother until she died on April 12, 2008. Talk about a forgiving heart.

Frances was anxious to leave that awful reality when she turned eighteen and moved to New Jersey, where she stayed with her Aunt Louise. She began working in a television manufacturing factory and met my father who was a handsome and seemingly worldly man. He subjected her to thirty-seven years of physical and psychological abuse to such an extent that it is hard to imagine. Mom finally found the courage to leave in December 1999, not long after Quinton was born. I still have ninety minutes of my dad's voice mails, threatening to kill me and my entire family if I didn't tell him where Mom was.

Ernest James Jackson was born in Mobile, Alabama, on August 28, 1936. I struggle to separate fact from fiction regarding his life, because he made up so many stories to appear larger than life or impress people. With that said, based upon what I have heard over the years from his side of the family, I may be able to provide a view of his life from a higher perspective. I believe my father, Quinton, and I were a lot alike when we were born. All three of us were innocent, genuine, and sweet boys; however, my father's world killed that part of him very quickly. My father grew up watching his mother prostitute herself and prostitute his sisters from time to time. From what I was told, he watched strong black men hung just for standing up against injustice and spent time homeless trying to take care of his sisters. My father lied about his age and joined the navy only to go AWOL after a period of time. At some point in his life, he obtained a second identity and went by Ernest Darden. I do not know if that had something to do with him going AWOL. For that matter, I am not even sure if that is what happened or if that is a story to cover for working undercover for the CIA or quite possibly him choosing to be estranged from his family—so many stories! For that matter, there is a distinct possibility that his birth name was Ernest Darden and that he changed it to Ernest Jackson before marrying Mom and back to Darden later in his life.

Over the years, he told us that he had played triple A baseball, played football for the Cleveland Browns, and boxed. Later in life, he claimed that he was a general in the marines; he even went so far as to buy a uniform and adorn it with bars and medals. At that point in his life, some people were on to him. However, it is no surprise that he created so many facades and stories after what he saw as a child.

He never believed he could just be who he was and be successful in life. He thought that he had to create different personas and become larger than life to open the doors of opportunity. And he did. Even with all the moments of pain and suffering, he could create opportunities and businesses through sheer force of will. We were never hungry. Nor did we ever lack a roof over our heads, but since he apparently never knew what unconditional love was, he was unable to give it to us.

This is the family I was born into on December 12, 1964, in East Orange, New Jersey. I was loved, there is no doubt about that. But I soon developed an interesting coping mechanism to deal with the reality I was living. One of my earliest memories is of seeing my mom fly through the air after being hit by my father. That memory is so fuzzy that I wonder if it even happened, but it did happen plenty of times later in life. At some point very early in my life, I climbed into a dream world to insulate myself from what I was seeing. I don't want to portray my life as all scary and violent. There were times when my existence was great, but the violence occurred frequently enough that this coping mechanism developed. It wasn't a conscious decision to daydream; it just happened. In my daydreams, I was typically a superhero like Superman, but more often I was Batman. I could daydream for hours. Additionally, some type of memory block must have been put in place, because there is a lot that I don't remember. It is like I was being protected in some way from being impacted by the violence and fear in my environment so I could follow a different path.

We moved to Freehold, New Jersey, in 1968. As I grew up, Dad installed a basketball hoop over the garage at my request. From 1972 to 1976, I spent much of my time shooting baskets. When I wasn't shooting hoops, I rode my bike and played with my best friend, Andrew Booth. I distinctly remember shooting hoops for hours, even in the rain, and I became good enough to make the all-star team while in fourth grade. I was so proud, but more than anything, I wanted my father to be proud of me. Unfortunately, it didn't work out quite the way I expected; my father walked out during the middle of a game, because he thought I was "playing like a pussy." During that same year when I was ten years old, I teased him that he looked pregnant; I quickly learned not to have fun at my father's expense.

As I grew, I became the peacekeeper and fix-it guy. We moved to Colorado in the spring of 1977. I was twelve years old and in sixth grade. After New Jersey, where I went to school in leisure suits and carried a briefcase while in elementary school, coming to Conifer, a mountain community forty miles southwest of Denver where kids wore jeans and T-shirts, was a shock. That first day of school in Colorado was traumatic; I remember coming home, begging my mom for jeans and T-shirts. My leisure suits and briefcase were immediately retired. On the other hand, moving to Conifer, Colorado, very quickly showed me how good humanity could be.

In New Jersey, I had been called a half-breed to my face while in second grade; it had been an eye-opening experience. Even though I avoided confrontation as a child, I went over the cafeteria table in an attempt to punch the individual. That was my introduction to racism. In New Jersey, people also did not wave to one another. So many that I came across had type A personalities. They were all rushing around to check their boxes, if you will.

In Conifer, I soon realized racism didn't exist, not that people even knew I was multiracial because I am so light-skinned and have straight hair. People were friendly. I distinctly remember being outside one afternoon when a neighbor, Glenn Trammel, drove by and waved. We hadn't met anybody yet. I had never experienced someone I didn't know waving to me. I froze; I didn't know what to do. By the time I figured out that I should wave back, he was gone. I waited all day outside, and when he drove past again, I waved enthusiastically. Soon, I realized that nobody in my immediate community cared that I wasn't quite white, and they only judged us on whether we were honest and worked hard. It was a breath of fresh air and has permanently endeared Conifer to me.

I took to maintaining our two acres without being told. I cut the grass around the property, dug drainage gullies in the driveway to prevent water from puddling, and maintained the garage. I was growing up and starting to establish my independence in small ways. When we weren't living in fear, after dinner we would all go downstairs and watch TV together. Both of my parents smoked, and I hated cigarette smoke. But I didn't dare say anything to them and risk my father's wrath. I began going to my room after dinner to either study or read, typically in my closet where I had a small desk with a light. About a year later, one of my parents asked why I wasn't watching TV with them after dinner anymore, and I explained that I could no longer stomach the smoke. They quit smoking shortly afterward but not without some fireworks; they discussed stopping together for some time. Eventually, Mom became impatient and stopped cold turkey, by herself. Dad was livid that quitting was not on his terms, but he grudgingly stopped as well.

During the first year in Colorado, we didn't have a basketball hoop, and it drove me crazy. I spent a lot of time simply sitting and watching the clouds. That was the point when my interest in the weather really took hold, but eventually I started pressuring my mom for a basketball hoop. At some point, Mom told my father. I must have been thirteen when my father called me downstairs. Before I reached the bottom of the stairs, he knocked me down by slapping me across the face. Apparently money was tight, and he didn't appreciate me asking for anything. Eventually though, he bought me a basketball hoop that I somehow managed to put up myself.

Ernie Jackson

While attending West Jefferson Junior High in Colorado, I continued to focus on my education and athletics—anything to further establish my sense of individuality and find my own path. Even then, I knew at my core that I didn't want to be like my father. I played football and basketball, ran track, and wrote articles for the *High Timber Times* about our athletic teams. I soon realized that I was a good athlete.

Once I was in high school, the administration impressed upon all of us the importance of college. I embraced this goal wholeheartedly and worked even harder, because I knew that I would get no help from my family. Or to be more truthful, I didn't want their help nor the strings that would come along with it. I became focused on obtaining a scholarship in football, and my reality began to change rapidly. Soon my father took notice. He wanted to be a part of my world, to share in my limelight. I really didn't care, because I had long been doing what I was doing for me and not for him. He cursed me once (well, probably more than once), as he asked me who had put me on a pedestal. Indeed, I was aloof, and as my sister Tina recently said, I was cold. I was desperately focused on surviving the abuse that my mom was experiencing (at an increasing frequency) and on getting out.

Tina wasn't the only one who felt that way. Mom wrote in her journal when our existence was its bleakest, specifically when she thought she would be beaten to death. The following are some of my mom's journal entries:

July 1980

This has been going on since the first year of our marriage. Keeping a record now because I fear for my life. I was beaten very badly last night, all night. Had cold water poured over me by the bucketful. Our girls' bedroom is directly above our bedroom, so they heard everything. Regina is very nervous, so she started to throw up as she does every time Ernest starts in on me.

As usual, he was accusing me of being with some man. His mother and sisters are or have been hookers at one time, so he thinks I am like them. Same topic every time he beats me up. My face is very badly swollen.

October 3, 1980

I spent the night behind the wood pile trying to keep warm. I walked out, because Ernest was accusing me of being with some man again. I was afraid to come inside. Heard all the children calling me, but was afraid to come home. I wanted to commit suicide but couldn't. Finally came inside at two thirty in the morning, freezing; slept in the bathtub until morning. Come morning, Ernest beat me very badly. He hit me with his fist, cutting my left eye, which left a permanent scar. Had to miss one week from work, which I took to keep us fed. He kicked and punched me all over. I am as sick as Ernest, because I let him do this to me. I cannot support these children alone, and if we split, he won't help. I know the children are as badly scared as I am; hopefully, one day they can get proper help. He always accuses me of having an affair and always says Tina is not his child, but she is. He even told her that he didn't want her around.

April 15, 1981

Ernie, Tina, and Regina:

So sorry to have to write this, but I have to. I love you all very much; you have kept me going all these years. Life has been hell for me. You three have been my little bit of joy. Today, I was beaten up again by your dad, because I saw Les Pendleton wave to us. He got very angry. It wasn't as bad as October 1980 but bad enough.

I have been a faithful wife to your dad, but he doesn't want to believe me. I hope you all go on to be successes in your lives. I thought I did a pretty good job as a mother to you all, but you will have to make up your own minds to that. Ernest told me if I quit the job as a cook at the elementary school, he was going to leave. He doesn't want me there, and he doesn't want me to quit. He accuses me of having an affair with somebody there. If I don't work, we don't have enough to eat.

Tina,

Always think of yourself as someone important. Don't ever believe that you are not. Don't let the boys take advantage of you. Be strong, which I am not. I was taken advantage of when I was twelve years old, and my life just fell apart. I have not been a strong person since then. Life is very cruel; you have to make it good for yourself in the right way. Always remember that.

I don't want to do what I am going to do, but there is no other way out for me. You can stick it out with everybody there or go to the state for help, but please don't live like I did. Look after Regina if you can; she will need the most help. She is too young to understand. Just tell her I loved her and I couldn't take the pain anymore.

Ernie,

I don't know why you dislike me so much. Maybe you believe all the things your Dad has accused me of. I have never slept around, even if he doesn't believe me; I want you to believe me. If you ever feel you have to beat up on a girl or someday your wife, please go for help from a doctor or just walk away. People are not to be beaten like animals. Ernie, you or Tina turn this over to the police if something happens to me.

Regina,

You are a dear, sweet girl, and I love you very much. I hope one day you will be very, very happy. Don't let anyone beat you like me. Go to somebody for help. I know you are suffering from all of this.

Quinton's Messages

To this day, I cannot remember the reality of this awful existence. Somehow through the grace of God, I blocked almost my entire childhood out. Forgetting was an effective way not to lose my mind or become like my father, but at what cost? As I read and type up my mom's journal entries, I am filled with anger. Why couldn't I do something? But I was just trying to survive.

I wonder if I did what I did around the house to make my father happy or because it needed to be done. In either case, I enjoyed my tasks. As I grew, when the unpleasantness became especially unbearable, I would remove myself by going for long runs, long bike rides, or long walks. When I started driving, I was reminded by Les and Cheryl Pendleton that I did the same with my sisters. I had forgotten. Les and Cheryl both told me that I often had both of them in the car with me. Tina called me the family patriarch, and I had that sense. This was long before I learned about auras and energy, but still I had a sense that I was trying to provide a calming influence, trying to fix the awful reality in some way. But I was a child. The violence toward Mom escalated to a point that, when I was fourteen, I felt moved to confront my dad about it. My father had begun going on runs with me, and one weekend day as we nearly finished, I found the nerve to ask him to stop hitting mom.

He turned to me and growled, "What? You are a man now?"

I whimpered and stammered, "No, I am not a man."

He stopped for a month, and then the abuse began again.

As I continued through high school, I was lonely and scared of getting my feelings hurt. I didn't know how to deal with girls. I was so socially backward. It was an interesting combination to be the starting quarterback, have my name in the papers, and yet not have the first clue about how to relate to girls. I consciously tried to keep everybody at arm's length by not smiling as I walked through the halls of Evergreen High School. I am certain that my father thought I was a homosexual; therefore, he did not object one little bit when I ordered a subscription to *Playboy* magazine when I was fifteen years old.

Ernie Jackson

While I had been in junior high and in eighth grade, I had made my mark in athletics and was fairly popular. A ninth-grade woman—she was not a girl in any sense of the word other than her age—became interested in me. The ninth-grade boys let me know and pressured me to ask her to go steady. This was the only time that I remember letting peer pressure get the best of me. After three weeks, I finally found the courage to hold her hand. I was so pleased with myself and happy. Not long afterward, she broke it off; she said, "I was expecting something more" than just holding hands. I was devastated and humiliated and swore it would never happen again. My whole life up to that point had been based upon preventing myself from being hurt by my family. I hadn't been prepared for this. I began eating lunch alone and recognized the peer pressure for what it was. In high school, I ate lunch in the weight room, behind the high school next to a creek, or in the middle of the football field—all in an effort to avoid my own social awkwardness and the feeling of being on the outside looking in.

The only fun I had was driving. My father had to beg to obtain an eight-hundred-dollar loan from a bank in Evergreen so we could buy a 1968 Camaro. I sat there as my father begged for this loan with tears in his eyes. Somehow, we scraped up enough money to buy my first car. It wasn't the prettiest on the outside, but it ran fast! It had a 327 small-block engine with a Rochester Quadra-Jet carburetor and a turbo 400 transmission. My father got me a job as a day porter in downtown Denver that summer, and the loan was repaid quickly.

I learned how to drive that summer and vividly remember the first time the extra two barrels of the carburetor opened. I was driving on Highway 74 and had just passed Evergreen Lake, where the road inclined. Somebody was driving slowly in front of me. As soon as I got to where the road widened to two lanes, I dropped the hammer. I floored the pedal and dropped the three-speed automatic to first gear. It felt like I was being thrown into the backseat as the car shot forward. What an adrenaline rush. I didn't drink and didn't know how to date, but I could drive! And drive I did my entire time in high school. Oddly enough, I did it without getting a traffic ticket in the Camaro. Looking back now, it seems I had a death wish. There was the time I went 120 miles per hour in a forty-five-mile-per-hour zone on Highway 73 in the fog and numerous other attempts to ask the question, "Is today my day to die?" I can remember actually asking the question as I accelerated at breakneck speed. I had no clue why I was on the planet, but no, it was not my time. I still had work to do.

After obtaining a football scholarship to the University of Wyoming, I left the house. It was after my freshman year, and I was finally beginning to grow from a boy toward being a man. I had a steady girlfriend who lived in Boulder who became my first wife, and we had decided to spend the summer together renting a room in a home. I came home to get whatever I valued—books, models, and I guess some clothes—which were all contained in a few boxes. The family was busy chopping and stacking wood, which was a task that I had always been an intricate part of. My father asked if I would lend them a hand, and I was so pleased to say no. I drove off. I wasn't very nice about it either, for I still could not stand up to my father. That would come about three years later.

I broke my leg in the fall intrasquad scrimmage while playing running back in my sophomore season. It took the trainers three days to realize I had broken my tibia in my left leg. I complained that something was clicking in my leg, and I still couldn't push off on the ball of my right foot. They finally took an X-ray and pronounced me a stud for walking around with a broken leg for three days. I was not a stud; it didn't hurt that badly. I ended up redshirting the entire season and was beyond angry about it. I was finally growing up and wanted to make my mark in the world.

The previous spring, I had been starting quarterback in drills. After playing on the scout team offense as a freshman at two hundred pounds as a scared little boy, I knew I was a punk. As soon as the season ended, I decided I wanted to add weight. I quickly put on twenty pounds by eating all the pizza and Doritos I could get my hands on. I had the sense that the coaches were concerned about my potbelly, but I quickly sculpted myself into a beast at 212 pounds during the off-season workouts. I came into spring as a physical specimen. One afternoon, while running the option during spring drills, the defensive end came toward me, and I pitched to the halfback. In case you didn't know, it is windy many days in Laramie, Wyoming. The ball floated in the wind, and for some reason, I didn't run after the loose ball. The quarterback coach ran up to me and started slapping me. Without a thought, I grabbed his elbows and may have lifted him off the ground. I didn't have malice in my heart; I just didn't want to be slapped, which is no surprise after growing up with my father. The next day, I was a running back. I don't think I was too happy about it, but I wanted to play and was in a better position to hit people. I had a sudden realization later that spring that I played my best football when I was trying to hurt the defenders. That thought stuck with me; I knew on some level that this could lead down a dangerous path.

After I missed most of the fall season of 1984, I was finally able to come back late in the season on scout offense. I was so unbelievably livid off about missing the season that in practice I was running first-team defensive players over every chance I got. One of the seniors let me know that wasn't cool. The guys were tired, had to play games on the weekend, and really didn't appreciate being run over in practice. They tried to tell me to back off, but I wouldn't listen. One of the guys eventually went after my newly healed broken leg. I limped off the field. The X-rays did not reveal a new break, but I was done, because once again I could not push off my leg. More than that, it broke my heart that my own teammates would do that to me, never mind that I was hurting them in practice. I was never the same, and years passed before I realized that, on some level, I may have had it coming. I would have hoped that I would come back even angrier, but something in my spirit broke. I came back in the spring in horrible shape and separated my shoulder because I was too slow to get around a wall of defenders. I walked away from football and my scholarship in the fall of 1985.

This time in my life was the proverbial fork in the road as I really began to grow faster toward manhood. It was painful and wondrous all the same. I stayed in Wyoming, and that fall, I landed a job on a road crew. I ran a jackhammer when we worked in the city and tried to run stakes for the grader when working on county roads, but I kept twisting my ankle. Winter set in, and I obtained a job at the local service station and often worked a graveyard shift. I don't remember how I landed either of these jobs, but I suspect my girlfriend, who worked as a waitress at the Village Inn, made the initial contact both times. I ran the cash register, changed oil, and repaired tires. It's funny now as I look back and realize that I enjoyed myself as I made $3.35 an hour. Winter was bitter cold, and I remember walking home one morning in negative forty degrees Fahrenheit. Eventually, the owners of the station discovered that I was multiracial, and our relationship went south rapidly, resulting in my loss of the job.

In the spring of 1986, my relationship with my girlfriend soured, and I moved out into a home that I rented for $175 a month. I had driven my car into the ground and needed a new motor. At that point, I was finally engaging in life, and I tried to get back on the road crew as spring approached. I was about to get back on the crew and had already priced the repair for the car when my dad called. I had stayed in contact with Mom, who never let on just how horrendous their existence was after I left, but she had my number and gave it to Dad. He had started his own janitorial business and needed somebody he could trust to supervise a cleaning crew in Phoenix. Despite our differences, he knew that, if nothing else, I was honest and hardworking. So I thought, *What to do? Keep on my path and make my own plan work or take what seemed like the easy way and run home to Daddy?* But my dad knew how to play me like a fiddle. He knew I needed to feel special; if he made it feel like I was doing him a favor, I would have a difficult time resisting.

I spent my early twenties desperately trying to be okay. I sought to define myself through work and was constantly looking for inner peace. I was striving to love and accept myself. I can say that now, but at the time, I didn't have a clue. I thought I was doing what I was supposed to be doing, but at times, I was just plain lost. While I had more success than failures professionally, my social life was a roller coaster. I guess for many of us, that is normal.

I reached a point in my early to mid-twenties (maybe I was twenty-three) when I became afraid of my anger. My temper had become more and more volatile over the years. I usually kept this part of myself private, but my father recognized it for what it was, and unbeknownst to me at the time, he started carrying a weapon with him whenever he was in my presence. It seems he had something to prove to himself. One night, he came to my home looking for a fight, and I was in the mood to beat him; to beat him like he had beaten my Mom so many times. It didn't take long for me to stride toward him with every intention of punching him in his face. Suddenly, he pulled a .357 Magnum out of his pocket and stuck it in my face. It was the proverbial moment of truth. I knew my father well enough to know that he wanted to evoke a fear reaction in me, which I refused to give him. We stood face to face, and I told him to pull the trigger. I think it made him proud on some level that I had stood up to him.

Kristine Jackson

Kristine Carole Cano is a wonderful woman, and I don't know if I will ever understand why she has stayed with me for as long as she has. Maybe I was her assignment before she was born into the physical realm. While I was a decent guy, I was still trying desperately to understand why I was here and what my purpose was before Quinton was called home, Kristine was not burdened with such matters, because she had already figured it out. Kristine must be an older soul than I am.

Ed Cano and Nellie Cano are Kristine's parents; Ed Jr. and Julie are her older siblings. She was born into their family of (now) five on July 23, 1972. Kristine was the youngest and might have been an accident, in that she wasn't planned. I guess that makes her a love child. Their family was not immune to the troubles that haunt so many of us, but theirs is a family that embodies love. Ed was family patriarch until he transitioned on June 8, 2003. Nellie always had his back and was loyal to the end.

Ed started hustling to provide money for his family when he was eleven years old, and he never stopped until the day he was called home.

Born February 10, 1944, Ed met Nellie when they were fourteen years old, and they were together ever since then. Ed's parents divorced when he was younger, so he had done what he could to earn money, including selling newspapers on the corner, eventually working in a men's clothing store, and then going into cabinetry and woodworking. Ed was more of a father to me than my own father was; I wish he were here for me to talk to now. Ed had a huge heart beneath his occasionally surly disposition.

Nellie is the consummate caregiver and provider.. Her mom, Eva, married Philip Redondo, and together they had four children. Nellie was the oldest, and she often heard her stepfather comment that she was lucky he had taken her in. Together, Ed and Nellie found love and acceptance when they married on August 18, 1963.

Together, they operated a bar and grill in Whittier, California, while Ed took a break from woodworking. Nellie cooked, and Ed made sure the atmosphere was lively. They were still in operation when Kristine was born, and she remembers the music playing, the lively atmosphere, and the dancing.

Ed and Nellie eventually tired of working so hard, and Ed began operating his own cabinet shop, but the pressures of finding the business and operating the shop took its toll. He told me on more than one occasion that he would lie awake at night, trying the figure out how to make ends meet. Ed swore it was the pressure of this existence that brought on type 2 diabetes. He eventually closed the shop and went to work for the union in Las Vegas.

Ed was a master wood craftsman and an excellent judge of character. He quickly made his way up the ladder to become shop foreman and ran numerous millwork finish jobs in the casinos. I was always amazed by his photo resume of projects he had completed and his stories. He commented to me that he would only have seconds to judge an applicant's character when he arrived at a project and hired a crew.

He saw something in me and allowed me to marry his daughter while quickly understanding my father's demons. We had many good times over the years and the retelling of those times could well be a book in itself. When all of us were together, all felt right with the world.

Ed's last lesson for me is yet another that I must have been intended to learn. On our last trip as a family to Rocky Point, Aunt Bertha and her daughters, Laura and Cathy, also attended. We had a blast eating and drinking in the restaurant. Although I was drunk, I carried Bertha up the stairs and deposited her in her wheelchair once back on level ground. We eventually made it back to our adjoining rooms. Kristine, Cheyanne, Quinton, and I were in one room, and Ed and Nellie were in the other. Ed couldn't find his wallet and became verbally abusive to Nellie. This whole episode hit a little too close to home for me. I sat on my bed listening and praying he would stop before I would have no choice but to make my presence known. I listened, knowing that my children, Kristine, Julie, her husband Tom, and their children were all hearing this as well. I was concerned that Cheyanne and Quinton would be negatively affected by what they were hearing and was amazed that nobody else would get involved. Finally, I walked into the adjoining room and said, "Ed, that is enough." Then he turned his attention to me, and then everybody got involved. Nellie was trying to hold Ed back, and everybody else was trying to hold me back. I had no intention of hitting Ed. But if he hit me, all bets were off, I rationalized as I tried to get closer to him.

In hindsight, this must have been a comical scene. Kristine said I must have had a flashback to all the abuse I had seen in my childhood. I think she is correct. I felt powerless to prevent the insanity in my father's house, but as a grown man, I was more than willing to stand up for what I thought needed to be done.

I shrugged off Kristine, Tom, and Julie as I kept walking forward toward Ed. Tom ended up on the ground, and he stuck his head between my knees and both of his arms around my legs. I couldn't move and briefly thought of balling up my fist and striking his skull, but I realized I would probably end up with a broken hand. Meanwhile, Nellie had somehow corralled Ed, and the freak show was over.

Quinton's Messages

I gathered Cheyanne and Quinton and took them out of the room and into the hallway. I sat down with them and wiped away their tears as I told them not to think poorly of Ed. They settled down, as did everybody else, and we all went to bed. For some reason, I slept on the floor; either Kristine was mad at me or I was mad at her. I was curled up on my left side when Ed came in early the next morning. He walked straight to me, knelt down, and said, "I am sorry. Please accept my apology for how I acted last night." What a man he was; I had never known a man to offer such a heartfelt apology. I halfheartedly accepted his apology, but I was never close with him again, and then he was gone one year later. I still regret not reconciling with him; he was indeed so much more of a man than I was at that time in my life. Ed offered a heartfelt apology within twelve hours of the incident, while I often held grudges for months or even years. What an idiot I can be. That lesson was learned . . . eventually.

Needless to say, Ed's transition was a nightmare for Kristine. We got the call late in the afternoon of June 6, 2003, right after we had finished planting four aspen trees in a newly constructed area of our yard that eventually became the sanctuary. Kristine, Cheyanne, and Quinton immediately flew to Los Angeles, where Ed had suffered a massive heart attack while walking from the ball field where TK was playing baseball to get something from his truck. He died as he wanted, without suffering. He fell to his knees and then backward onto his back. The doctors kept him on life support until Kristine got there, and they all gathered around him to say their good-byes. Quinton sat on Grandpa Ed's lap as he had always done, without really understanding what was happening. I wasn't there, because I apparently felt I needed to wrap up something at work before heading that way. Then I drove, preferring to be alone as I grappled with my emotions and regrets.

Ed's service was very moving. The church in Whittier, California, was packed with those whose lives had been touched by Ed—family, friends, coworkers, and clients. There was so much love as all of us celebrated his life. I shed a tear, which was monumental. I was so pinched off from my emotions that shedding a tear for my father-in-law felt right and well overdue. More would come, but that first tear was big, especially since no tears were shed when my own father passed away a little over three months later.

The immediate family went up to the podium, offering a few words each. I remember my brother-in-law, Tom Ochoa, speaking. I found myself behind the microphone in front of hundreds of people that I didn't know and who didn't know me. I had something to say.

"Edgar Cano wouldn't have had it any other way," I said. "Ed had told me that he did not want to die a piece at a time." He got his wish; he didn't suffer. One second he was there, and the next he was pure energy.

Kristine and me . . . our lives together epitomized philosophical differences about living in the moment, and she was more right than I was. Kristine always did and continues to live in the moment. She never really did worry about money; if she wanted to do something or buy something for someone to show her love, she did so. Meanwhile, I was the exact opposite, forever budgeting and watching the money, cautious to leave some of it for later. Kristine would always say that tomorrow wasn't promised and that I might not ever get a chance to spend it. Categorize it any way you want, but she was right, as we have learned together. Tomorrow is not promised, and we need to start appreciating each and every moment, each and every sunrise and sunset, each and every smile, each time we connect with another human being, each butterfly, each hummingbird, and on and on. Of course, that doesn't give us a license to spend ourselves into bankruptcy, but we need to stop worrying so much about the next dollar bill and start enjoying our time here.

Cheyanne Jackson

How do I describe my now eighteen-year-old daughter? As I sit here, her entire life is playing out before my eyes. She was such a sweet and beautiful baby, a sweet and beautiful child, and a beautiful young woman who is difficult to relate to at times. Cheyanne rarely cried as a toddler. She was almost always happy and secure in herself. She enjoyed being with both of her parents. Waking up in the morning to feed her was consistently the brightest part of my day. Those early morning smiles and our time together . . . well, they were precious. Memories of putting her into bed with Kristine as I left for the gym or left for work are fond.

In our first home on Thirty-Eighth Avenue and Sweetwater, Ed finished the remodeling I had started, and then we had the perfect little starter home. Cheyanne's room was beautiful, but we still didn't have a pool, which made the Phoenix summers a little warm, if you know what I mean. That didn't stop Cheyanne and I; we would lounge around in the backyard in our swim trucks and take turns running through the sprinkler.

Our next house was a larger trilevel. Shortly after we moved in, we had a pool installed, and at eighteen months of age, she learned to swim. Cheyanne never had any issues with the stairs. By the time we moved in she crawled and walked all over. Ever the life of the party, she would turn to one of us and announce that she was going to bed when she became tired. Or she would just wander off only to be discovered sleeping at the top of the stairs as if she just couldn't go any farther.

We spent a lot of time in the backyard. Not long after we moved in, I built a two-part structure in the corner of our backyard. It was part shed and part playhouse for Cheyanne. She played in there when it wasn't blazing hot (meaning in the winter, spring, and fall).

I still remember sweat beading beneath her curly hair. Cheyanne essentially had no hair for about two years, just some fuzz on top, and then she suddenly had an afro! She has hair most women would die for, and now she often straightens it to look like everybody else's. However, at times now, she will just wash it and let it go naturally into such beautiful curls.

Life was perfect for Cheyanne until we moved away from Kristine's family to where my heart called home in Conifer, Colorado. Fifteen months after that traumatic change, she was suddenly no longer an only child. I was ever so conscious of trying to be with both of my children, but it was simple math. Cheyanne went from being the center of our world to having to share the spotlight with Quinton. While so many of us experience this, I still don't think on some level, Cheyanne has completely gotten over it.

I had such hopes for Cheyanne. Although I grew up shy, introverted, and withdrawn, I prayed that Cheyanne would be different. For a while, it seemed that she was, and then something changed. While she was still loving, somehow she became self-conscious and somewhat withdrawn. *How could that be?* I wondered. She never had to live in fear or watch her father beat her mother. Maybe part of our shared experience is genetics. I eventually came out of my shell, and I expect she will too; in fact, I think she is beginning to right at this very moment. Cheyanne is becoming so much more opinionated and assertive. It is like she too is getting the message and trying to make the most of every moment, but she is still a teenager who sometimes leaps before she thinks.

As so many of us with teenage children know, the children become unrecognizable at times, and Cheyanne isn't any different. It was next to impossible for me to relate to her. I was unable to get beyond that fact that "I wasn't like that when I was her age." I wondered, *So why is she?*

We had another obstacle, we came to find out. As all of us find ourselves living a different normal, we have been blessed with meeting people whom we probably would not have met if our son hadn't transitioned back to pure energy at such a young age. Quinton's departure from the physical realm and subsequent visitation challenged us to expand ourselves. In our travels, Cheyanne has discovered that she may be, on some level, a psychic and therefore more perceptive to other people's energy. While I don't know if she will ever develop this ability, I think it hurt our relationship; invariably, I would come home from work either with negative energy or with no energy at all. She would key in on that and go the opposite direction.

With Quinton's transition, my relationship with my daughter is headed back to what it was. Kristine did most of the parenting previously, because I tended to overreact, but Kristine forever tried to be Cheyanne's friend too. Recently, as I have become more aware of my energy, especially in terms of how I communicate with Cheyanne, our relationship has improved. I still have to be a parent, but I can do so with love.

Our relationship aside, my observations of Cheyanne through the years have shown her to be caring and thoughtful. Oftentimes, Cheyanne would wade into her friends' dramas and dispense some amazingly profound advice. I look forward to watching Cheyanne grow into a strong, intelligent young woman, all the while having a loving father/daughter relationship with her.

Summary

Seconds have turned into minutes, minutes into hours, days, weeks, and then years; time seems to be moving quicker and quicker. Much has happened since Quinton was called home. For that matter, much has happened since I started this book.

With the messages we received and the lessons we learned, I, for one, now realize that I am truly not in control of the big picture. Naturally, I still have free will and what is deemed a responsibility to make the most of every moment. This surrender, if you will, has led to experiences that I never thought I would have, and contained within these experiences are lessons to be learned and knowledge to be shared. The knowledge sharing is on a two-way street. Let me explain.

Sharing

I have continued to share our experiences with those who seem interested yet I have to be careful. There have been a handful of times when I have begun to share and immediately sensed a distinct lack of interest. After some experiences with people who really aren't interested, I have begun to realize that I am here to do more than just share, so as time has passed, my intent to share has waned a bit, but that isn't to say I don't share anymore. In fact, while my intent to share has waned, sometimes I find myself sharing even more.

This has come about because I find myself stretched thin across the various responsibilities that I have accepted since Quinton was called home. These responsibilities or tasks include my job with Prime West, coaching football, writing this book, my responsibilities as president-elect of BOMA Denver, working with the district attorney to reduce the charges against the young lady who ran us over, and working with our attorney as we slowly move toward settling our insurance claims associated with the accident. Because I am stretched thin, I am less in my head and a little more open to experience what is going on around me; I end up sharing with people who not only are interested but have had similar experiences. Meeting these like-minded individuals keeps me on the more spiritual path.

As time has passed, another sensation has emerged. Within the context of my new tasks and responsibilities, I meet a lot of people. As I meet them, I realize that they don't even know Quinton; they don't know of our loss or our experiences. What is more, sometimes I sense that they really don't care. Please note that these are just impressions in my mind, but it still saddens me. There have been other times when I get the impression from people who know me well that some might be a little impatient with me, wondering when I might move on or "get over it" as had been said to others who have suffered losses. Again, these are just impressions that are imprinted somewhere in my mind at times. When I have these impressions or invariably meet someone who says it to my face, I know I will smile and ask "Why?" Quinton has set me on the most wonderful journey of enlightenment, and I know that he not only exists by the signs he sends occasionally but that I will see him again. This frames my perspective on life, and within this context, most of information we are bombarded with in the media has ceased to have meaning. This is a gift as well.

Football

One of the football coaches from when I played at Evergreen High School came to me before Quinton's service. As I lay on the couch in my family room, probably with an ice pack on my leg, Coach Mike Carter leaned over, whispered in my ear, and said in a gravelly voice, "When are you going to stop effing around and do what you are supposed to do?" My eyes must have opened wide as I asked what he meant. He explained that I was supposed to be coaching football. I was at a loss for words. I had walked away from the game twenty-four years earlier and essentially never looked back. Mike was emphatic and, from my perspective, knew something about me that I was unaware of.

Jenifer Mintle was at our home that night, and she pounced and never let it go. Jenifer had the unenviable task of getting me, who can be as dense as they come, and the head football coach to meet. She worked at this for up to nine months. Jenifer kept at me and eventually got me excited at the prospect of coaching, even when I felt completely lost after spending a week with the team during the month of October 2009. Even though I became excited at the prospect, the phone didn't ring, and I began to think it wasn't meant to be. I mean, I had been away from the game for so long, and I really didn't know what to expect anyway.

Coach Molholm met me for breakfast in April of 2010, and he made a formal offer. I accepted because of Mike Carter's and Jenifer Mintle's convictions, while I continued to be in a state of disbelief that I would actually be coaching. I rationalized that the least I could do was have the courage to try; if it didn't go well, I could bow out at the end of the season.

By the third day of spring camp, I was beginning to feel that I could benefit the young men. That moment came during a drill I was present for; suddenly, I was coaching. It was an epiphany. I emphatically shared my knowledge of the game and my positive energy. As I did so, a little voice in the back of my head said, *Don't look now, Jackson, but you are coaching.*

It was a magical year. I shared life lessons and harped on the value of hard work and simply believing in one's self. We won eight games during the regular season and only lost two after losing seven the year before. But I was still a little slow; I thought what was going on between me and the team was happening one way. By the fourth game of the season, I finally realized that it was a symbiotic relationship and that I was receiving their love and positive energy as much as, if not more than, I was sharing mine with them. When I awoke one morning with this realization, I cried tears of joy.

I continue to juggle work (I returned to commercial property management, but this time with Prime West) and football. I leave work early one day a week during the off-season to help with the off-season lifting program and twice a week during the season. The players on the team continue to lift my spirits and I theirs.

Still, Kristine and Jenifer say it best in terms of what my involvement with the team means to my family and to the team. With tears in her eyes, Kristine shared that being an assistant football coach brought the light back into my eyes. She hadn't known if it would ever return. And after growing frustrated with me for not being able to articulate what coaching meant to me, Jenifer replied to my statement that I "may have made a difference in some of their lives," by rolling her eyes and sharing what the young men said about me. According to Jenifer, they said, "Coach Jackson got us to believe in ourselves." There is no greater gift than knowing my part in making a positive impact on these young men.

Reading

I continue to read what many term "new age" and explore metaphysics and even a little quantum physics (about the way our consciousness affects the behavior of subatomic particles) in my effort to understand the fact that Quinton exists and continues to send us signs. The implications of what I am reading are mind-blowing, but they do not take away from what I am clearly intended to learn in my life. I look forward to continuing this journey of enlightenment as I prepare for my own transition someday, but there is something profound that I must share.

There are simple and universally known common themes that I have picked up from my reading of new age material, those being the importance of love, gratitude, appreciation, and simply put, positive energy. While I have been reading and sharing, many friends have come to me. Some people feel strongly that the way to salvation is only through Christ. Well, I have been reading the New Testament as well—yes, finally reading the red print! What is profound to me is that much of the new age I have read seems to tie directly back to the words of

Jesus Christ. One verse from the *New Living Translation Bible*, Matthew 17:20, continues to resonate with me. It says, "'I tell you the truth, if you had faith even as small as a mustard seed, you could say to this mountain, 'Move from here to there,' and it would move. Nothing would be impossible.'"

Indeed. Have faith and don't be afraid, Jesus repeated over and over. What a gift these words are.

Listening and Surrendering

I took an extended amount of time off. After trying to come back to work a second time during the last quarter of 2009 and eventually resigning, I didn't work from January through the middle of May 2010. In about April, I realized that I would have to go back to work at some point in the future. While I was having a lunch with a friend, within the week, I was offered an assistant general manager position on her staff and in the same field of commercial property management that I had been working in for ten years. I accepted, which I never would have done in the past, because she was a friend. Now I was less concerned about what I could not control, so I accepted, started on May 24, 2010, and hoped for the best.

In this new position, I shared all of my knowledge, which saved the property tens of thousands of dollars. I often joked that I was sharing all that I knew, and then it would be time for me to leave; I was joking, but my comments ended up being prophetic. Not long after I started, Kristine stopped working her part-time job, and it took me at least three months to realize that I wasn't covering the expenses of our Colorado and Arizona homes. Interestingly, when I realized this, I didn't panic and didn't discuss it with anyone. I just said to myself, "Well, let's see what happens." I rationalized that I could always pull money out of my long-term investments to hold us over until Cheyanne graduated from high school, or we could sell the Colorado home and move into our Arizona home. I had also given my word to my friend and her manager that I would stay awhile, so I was in no hurry to break that promise, even though it was going to cost me money. Well, the universe had different ideas.

Within a week of me realizing that my salary wasn't covering our expenses, a couple of pretty amazing things happened. First, I was nominated as the BOMA Denver Principal Member of the Year, which was totally unexpected. The Denver chapter is over ninety years old and a very prestigious organization. It was quite an honor to be nominated for the award, let alone to win it, but this was a precursor of more to come. Second, the phone rang with a job offer more in line with my experience and what I had been doing in my career recently. Having surrendered completely to God's will—I immediately recognized the significance of the offer. I interviewed and hit it off with the owner. Upon our next meeting, they made their offer, which would have meant a raise of twenty-thousand dollars per year, contingent upon me removing the earring from my ear. It took me a second, but not much longer, to realize that the universe had presented me with an opportunity to demonstrate just who I was, and I beamed inwardly and outwardly. I explained with love and gentleness the significance of Quinton's earring. I shared that I was wearing it to honor my son and hadn't taken it out since putting it in. After that meeting, I was walking on cloud nine with the knowledge of who I had become. I was exuberant. Within two days of me officially learning that the job offer had been rescinded, Prime West offered me a senior property manager position. Knowing me and the significance of Quinton's earring, they didn't make their offer contingent upon its removal. I gave my two-week's notice and started with them on October 11.

Again, the significance of this turn of events wasn't lost on me. The universe had spoken clearly and left me with the distinct impression that I was intended to stay in Colorado indefinitely. Just in case I wasn't clear, I received another phone call, this one from the prior year's BOMA Denver president. This call was to ask me if I would accept their nomination to be president-elect for the year 2012. Really? The old Ernie would have felt unworthy, insecure, and too afraid of failure to even consider accepting. But I accepted for the same reasons that I had accepted the coaching position; with everything I had experienced, I knew that I had little say in the matter because I had surrendered control. If others felt that strongly that I should do it, then at least I could have the courage to accept. So I did.

Closing

As I put the finishing touches on this labor of love that has taken me longer than I expected, I find myself pulled in many directions and appreciative of all of them. I am more enlightened, more appreciative of every breath, more taken by a smile from anyone (especially a child), and acknowledging of every message Quinton sends me. I go through life more in the moment than ever, but please don't think I am perfect. I still am occasionally tired, and maybe even cranky, as I carry on my Tasmanian devil impersonation at times, trying to accomplish what it seems like I am supposed to accomplish. But there is more to this seemingly perpetual state of busyness.

I believe the universe has placed me within this lifetime in an effort for me to finally get it. There is so much more than just doing for the sake of doing or than checking boxes. So many of you know this, but I am only internalizing it now, and I hope to use my remaining time in a state of being, in an enjoyment of every moment without fear. I believe that within this state of busyness lies the catalyst to finally, once and for all, tear down the walls that I have hidden behind for so long and, in doing so, allow myself to be vulnerable.

Beyond that, what comes next is out of my hands. I could lose my job tomorrow and leave property management all together or not. Who knows? But I am enjoying this state of physical being more now than ever before and most importantly, this nightmare and journey of revelations has brought Kristine and I closer together.

Afterword

We miss our beloved son, brother, and friend. There are no two ways about it. It is difficult knowing that I am forced to live the rest of my life without him. I had so looked forward to watching him grow into manhood, but now all of that is gone. In its place is a new knowledge associated with a new path that he set us upon and a new perspective. As we go through our new lives, the things we once thought were important are now meaningless.

I often laugh to myself when, as I go through each day, I ask the question, "You mean you expect me to get excited, nervous, or concerned about this silliness?" But all the while, the entire journey of my life—all of it—seems scripted or planned out, which is why I included so much about who I was and who we were before our worlds were turned upside down and the light of our lives was called home. It is hard to fathom such a journey filled with the contrast of fear, hate, and anger with love, peace, and acceptance. On the wings of this contrast comes a message intended to share.

How do we distill this down to something resembling a sound bite? I don't know that it is possible, but it starts with learning to be love instead of fear, hate, or envy. Love yourself enough to allow yourself to love others. Have you ever noticed that, when you are filled with love and peace within yourself, people are drawn to you? It is quite the occasion to be walking through life with good energy that may or not manifest itself on your lips as a smile and to see your good energy's impact upon others as they make eye contact and send a smile in your direction. In those moments, you truly feel connected to something larger than all of us. All of this and more, Quinton illustrated as he walked through his life in the physical realm with us. He did it consistently, without pretense, and then the messages began.

As described within this text, Quinton clearly and unequivocally made his presence known after he transitioned to pure energy. He is not gone, whatever "gone" means. In the small sampling of people whom we have been in contact with who have lost loved ones, it is almost unanimous.

Maybe I should use the rest of my life to bring these occurrences to light. Look at what we have been shown. We have been shown that there is so much more to our existence than we are led to believe. Now what will you do with this knowledge? What does it mean for you? I suspect that many of you already know; you quietly live your lives in love and peace, enjoying every moment with friends, family, acquaintances, and strangers with whom you connect. As I travel this new path, I meet more and more people who don't even have TVs in their homes and have cancelled the newspaper. In doing so, they have removed what may be the predominant source of our fears, our envy, and our insecurities. Once those feelings abate, love and peace remain.

I have love for you. I love you enough to share our journeys and Quinton's messages. I send you all my energy, all my love.

God bless you, and be well, as you are intended to be!

Acknowledgments

We would like to thank all our family, friends, and neighbors. This list includes our current and former coworkers, tenants, and employers—so many in these categories are, in effect, friends. We send special thanks to the mountain communities of Conifer and Evergreen and to all of our friends with the Denver metropolitan chapter of the Building Owners and Managers Association.

Special thanks go to those listed below who came to our aid in June of 2009:

All of the nurses and doctors at the San Juan Regional Medical Center in Farmington, New Mexico, and the Southwest Memorial Hospital in Cortez, Colorado

Layla Voldrich
Barney Carter, paramedic
George McNeil, paramedic
Doug and Leah Bedker, Doug's Quality Towing
Jim and Troy Redondo
Mike and Chris Voldrich
Alex and Renee Brister
John and Tracey McDonough
Les, Cheryl, and Stacey Pendleton
Jeff Goldman
Doug and Tracey Wills
Bob Stedman
Troy and Cathie Nicholson
Colin and Kathryn Price
Jon and Sally Lapham

Quaid and Emi Pauls
Lewis Mortuary in Evergreen, Colorado
Ertel Funeral Home in Cortez, Colorado
Our Lady of The Pines church in Conifer Colorado.

ABOUT QUINTON'S LEGACY

In the spring of 2015, I published a second book about our son Quinton. To give you an idea of its content, I've enclosed the introduction to that second book that is available on amazon.com and also as an eBook.

INTRODUCTION TO QUINTON'S LEGACY

So much has happened since the publication of *Quinton's Messages*. Much of it is amazing and all of it with purpose. The journey has continued and while the extraordinary has become common place, still I want more. More visits, more signs, more sharing of our message!

My friend John McDonough, who is a poet, photographer and philosopher, and my wife, Kristine, helped me crystalize the message I share with people who have lost a loved one or are searching for greater meaning in life. I use it in my standard signature for *Quinton's Messages*: "What we are dealing with is not a matter of believing or a belief. We are dealing with knowledge; know *there is more*!"

This book, *Quinton's Legacy*, is the sequel and written primarily for those who read the first book. *Quinton's Legacy* has three sections.

The first section is the story of our journey to forgiveness, Quinton's visits with us, messages from Quinton via renowned medium Rebecca Rosen, discovering my guardian angel and reconciliation with my deceased father. We continue to discover what "*there is more*" means for us.

Section two includes stories from others who have experienced visits from deceased loved ones—messages from beyond the grave. We also discovered that when our pets transition, it is possible for them to be here for us also. Now that the door has been opened, the revelations that once filled me with awe, amazement and reverence have become the norm; my eyes are opened to how the world works. If these ideas are new to you, buckle your seat belts, you are about to go for a ride.

In section three practical advice is given. We go beyond merely reporting the Divine experiences that have blessed us to share a broader perspective; a snapshot of what I have come to believe. You see, in opening the door to *there is more*, all of us are invited to learn and embrace new way of thinking about life and death. I share my perspective, in general terms, from our family's experiences since Quinton's transition, as well as those who have crossed our paths. We note multiple sources to further illustrate that these experiences are not unique; they occur so frequently, they're commonplace.

Yes, what we have experienced is an amazing peek inside the workings of the universe. With that said, the purpose of *Quinton's Messages* and this sequel is to pique your interest enough to do your own research. The experiences we share, along with this information can be found from the internet, bookshelves or first-hand. All that is required is to slow down from time to time and take note of what you are experiencing, and then acknowledge it for what it is.

Enjoy the journey and in knowing there is more.

Made in the USA
Middletown, DE
12 December 2020